Out of the Blur:

A Delirious Dad's Search for the Holy Grail of Work-Life Balance

by James Sudakow

illustrated by Todd Kale

**PURPLE
SQUIRREL**
MEDIA GROUP

Purple Squirrel Media
San Diego, California
www.purplesquirrelmedia.net

Print ISBN: 978-0-9965033-0-3

Electronic ISBN: 978-0-9965033-3-4

For my wife

Table of Contents

Part I: "The Blur"

Work-Life Balance: Reality, Myth, or Urban Legend? The Humble Search Begins

When my sister and I were young, we couldn't understand why our dad spent so much time in coma-like naps on the family room floor every weekend. The loud snoring, which otherwise would have been annoying, was reassuring because at least we knew he was still alive. We were also amused by how much time he spent in the bathroom. What was wrong with him? Fortunately, he always emerged as the same healthy dad we knew and loved before he went in there a half hour earlier. I don't have any hard proof, but to this day, I think my dad frequently combined the two and was napping *in* the bathroom.

Decades later, as a fully grown "real" adult, who is now a husband and dad who founded and now runs a successful boutique business consulting practice, I have an acute appreciation for my dad's odd behaviors. Sometimes, when you try to balance everything that work and life throw your way, you end up so tired that lying face first on the family room floor—or for me, the hard tile of the kitchen floor—feels surprisingly comfortable. As for the bathroom, it turns out that my dad knew a secret that I wouldn't learn until the time was right: the bathroom might be the last place left on earth where you can get a little time away from everything. A group of dads back in history must have realized this and formed some sort of dad real estate collective because today dads have unquestionably cornered the market on the bathroom. You might as well rename it "Dad's refuge." In his day, my dad probably used it to read the newspaper or just think. In my day, it's about those things, too, although technology adds checking e-mails, texting, and maybe playing a round of my Home Run Derby baseball game app—all with the intent to compose myself for the work-life chaos that awaits outside the safe confines of this sacred room.

As a kid, I was too young to realize the high degree of difficulty required to successfully execute the work-life balance maneuver my dad pulled off every day. As my first boss used to tell me, "Never let them see how the sausage is made." My dad never did. He made it look easy. He ran the West Coast operation of a small business. Despite working long hours, traveling, and having to be on daily conference calls with the East Coast parent company at 6:00 every morning, he somehow also managed to be home for dinner almost every night; coach my Little League baseball teams; and help with science projects, math homework, and whatever else I needed. He did similar things for my sister, not to mention the long list of things I'm sure he did for my mom that we kids were blissfully unaware of. To do it all, I later found out that he went to bed at about midnight every night and woke up at 4:30 every morning like clockwork. If this was an Olympic event, we'd be looking at a degree of difficulty equivalent to those crazy platform dives that only the divers from the Chinese Olympic team are allowed to even attempt let alone execute with any kind of grace. My dad worked like a dog to run his business, worked like a dog to be a good dad, and worked like a dog to be a good husband. We were the benefactors of it all, something that I'm sure made him proud when he thought about it for thirty seconds before passing out on the family room floor two minutes into a baseball game.

For the last ten years, I've been faced with the same challenges my dad faced. Like dads these days, though, our challenges exist in the technology age, where no one can hide anywhere anymore, including the bathroom. And despite the technological advances that are marketed to make our lives easier and more efficient, a lot of us seem to be working really long hours (which now often includes working in the bathroom) as companies run tighter and leaner by asking us to do more with less. Not that I needed any more respect for my dad than I already had, but when I first realized what it took to pull this off, I gave him a little extra nod from the car as I drove past the cemetery where he now rests. Sometimes, I stop and thank him personally. I suspect at some point my own kids are going to wonder why *their* dad sleeps a lot in his chair while resting his head on the dusty window sill. As a business owner and a dad, I care enormously about my work and even more enormously about my family. Balancing them often feels like an impossible dream. I've been trying hard every day to turn that impossible dream into a possible reality. It has put me on the search for the holy grail of work-life balance for some time now, and I've often wondered if anybody else has yet figured out this diabolical puzzle.

My search started where many quests start in the technology era: on Google. I typed in "work-life balance" and was simultaneously relieved and overwhelmed that my search yielded 29 million results in 0.7 seconds. At least I wasn't alone in looking for help. There were a lot of experts offering widely varying solutions. Some offered ideas like "37 Tips on How to Get Better Work-Life Balance." If I had time to read thirty-seven ways to improve my work-life balance, I probably didn't have a work-life balance problem in the first place. I read the article anyway. At least one of the thirty-seven tips had to apply to me. Other articles took on a more draconian feel, arguing that work-life balance was a false reality and that our pointless quest was part of what created our stress about work-life balance in the first place. They recommended giving up on it. Accept that there is no such thing as work-life balance. Replace it with a more realistic work-life *blend*. What did that mean? It seemed that this blended approach meant something like taking your kids to work and trying desperately to keep them distracted and quiet while you conducted conference calls and meetings. I wanted no part of that work-life reality. I wasn't capable of that kind of multitasking. I was still trying to master doing conference calls and sending e-mails at the same time. No way were kids entering that equation without causing a disaster. It would be only a matter of time before my kids escaped the confines of the conference room in which I had them sequestered, inevitably finding their way into the executive board room to interrupt a sensitive meeting.

Then I came across an article that felt starker: "Work, Family, Friends, or Health. Choose Two." If I understood this one correctly, I could choose one of several options of which none were any good. I could have work and family but be unhealthy and friendless. Or I could be healthy with a great job but live a lonely life of solitude. Or I could have a great family and lots friends but no money. At least in the last version, I'd have couches to squat on since I had so many friends. I deleted that article even though in the back of my mind, I acknowledged the author's legitimate point about choices and prioritization.

After a lot of reading and still not feeling like I had any idea how to improve my work-life balance, I moved beyond Google. First, I listened to podcasts and radio shows about entrepreneurs who were also parents. Unfortunately, to add to my growing concern, many of the hosts and guests also believed that there was no such thing as work-life balance. "All we have are choices," they said. That seemed a bit too transcendental for me, although I have to admit that I have no idea what transcendental means. The more I read and listened, the more I was beginning to understand how we got to this notion of work-life blend. I still wasn't about to give up on the idea that work-life balance wasn't a mirage or urban legend. It had to exist. I remembered a guy who worked for one of my clients. Darryl from Accounts Payable seemed to have found the secret. He was married. He had kids. He had a good job. He was always coming back from vacation. He was a real person who was doing all of these things, though his constant vacationing might explain why my invoices took so long to process. Regardless, Darryl from AP was a happy, mellow, and employed dad. What did Darryl from AP know that the rest of us didn't? One day I asked him, to which he responded: "I don't know. I enjoy my life." That sounded nice and easy. Too nice and easy. If there was one lesson I had learned in life so far, it was that when things seem really easy, they are never really easy. People who are really good at things just make the rest of us think those things are more readily attainable than they might really be. Maybe Darryl from AP was a work-life balance savant who knew how to achieve work-life balance but had absolutely no idea how he was doing it.

I asked other dads I knew about the keys to work-life balance. Some laughed and asked me to tell them the answer if I ever found it. Others bought into the work-life blend approach. One even told me that his entire company had adopted work-life blending. Finally, I talked to a neighbor from down the street who had just retired. He had married and raised kids, then remarried and raised more kids, all while holding seemingly important jobs along the way. He always seemed to be in a good mood. He had to know something. When I asked him about work-life balance, he smiled and told me to go five blocks down the street, make a right, and the answer would be on the corner. Had the holy grail of work-life balance been in my own neighborhood the whole time? I knew sometimes I didn't see things right in front of my face—something my wife regularly reminds me of when I stand in front of the open refrigerator searching for the cheese. How could I have missed something as big as the answer to my work-life balance question, though? I followed my neighbor's directions and ended up at Starbucks. Had he misunderstood my question? Or was he just amusing himself at my expense in his retirement years? Then again, maybe he was on to something. Was the key to work-life balance upping my caffeine intake? I hoped not. I don't like coffee.

After all of this searching, I had a lot of information but was no closer to figuring out how to achieve some semblance of balance. All the while, I kept cranking through each day, trying to do everything on all fronts with no real plan for how to do it. My life started to feel like a work-life blur more than anything else. I wasn't unhappy; I was just in a haze—one that was beyond the general haze that my wife proclaimed I had always been in, even before kids came into the picture. Some days, I made it through the haze and got everything done without incident. I had no idea how that happened. More frequently, my days felt like one calamity after another. I had no idea how *that* happened. I had to do something. The question was where and how to start. I needed a well-thought-out methodology instead of just a random selection from the thirty-seven tips in that article I had read.

And then one day, I was driving home after a meeting with a client who I was assisting with some sizable company-wide transformational changes. I often used my drive time to zone out and contemplate whatever floated into my head. On nights when I was really tired, I zoned out about admittedly ridiculous things, such as pondering whether I would have taken the red pill or the blue pill if I had been Neo in the movie *The Matrix*. That night, my thoughts bounced back and forth between my client's business situation and my work-life balance problem. The two topics spun around together in my head for a while and resulted in me asking myself an unexpected but thought-provoking question:

> *If my life were a business and I was my own business client, what would I advise myself to do to fix my work-life problem?*

At first, I wondered if my overabundance of research into work-life balance had finally caused my brain to malfunction and concoct a farfetched connection between my client and my life. But the more I thought about it, the more I realized that the idea of applying business transformational strategies to my work-life balance situation wasn't so halfcocked and might have some legitimate merit. After all, thinking about work-life balance this way couldn't be any more futile than what I had already tried, and at least I knew business transformation methodology. Could this same approach help me achieve a sustainable work-life balance? I decided to give it a try.

And that is what this book is about. What started as a question seemingly out of left field evolved into a systematic approach for solving my work-life balance problem. This book explains the methodology that ultimately got me to a healthier, more satisfying way of living. To illustrate my methodology, I'll let you see my own personal story and journey—one that spanned a full year. You'll see that my former life was often comical and absurd enough for me to wonder if I was actually a cartoon dad who just thought he was a real person, meaning you'll get a few laughs at my expense. It's okay to laugh. I've got thick skin. I work in the business world. And if I remember my college life well enough, one guy laughing at another guy was often just a way of saying that they were friends. I also reveal the many course corrections I made over the year. I do this because my discovery process was just as important as my results. I didn't get things right the first time in many cases. You may gain some insights from my blunders; in other words, you can learn from my mistakes.

Some of my story and life may look and feel a lot like yours. I work in the business world. I worked my way up through the years from data entry clerk to vice president and then started my own business eight years ago. I'm happily married with two great kids—a new baby boy and a two-year-old boy. Some of my story may not look like your life. On top of our own two kids, my wife and I are legal guardians for her younger brother and sister, who are now sixteen and twenty. We're not their parents but have been in a formal parental role for them for a decade. So essentially, we've got teenagers and toddlers all inhabiting the same family ecosystem. Sometimes, that ecosystem is really cool and unique.

Sometimes, it feels like a powder keg. And, of course, we have eight chickens, a dog, and a rabbit. Why? Most of the time, I have no idea. What you and I most likely have in common is that we are trying to solve the same problem: how to be successful in our work and be very much an active part of our families. Because our lives may be similar in only some ways and inevitably different in other ways, as I tell my story, I will frequently pause throughout the book to offer you specific and practical ways to apply what I've learned to your own lives—how to create your own work-life vision, how to identify any specific traps that might be getting in your way, and even how you can solve some of the traps most of us face every day.

I should probably throw out a disclaimer (no book would be complete without at least one). I'm a dad and husband writing this book from a dad and husband's point of view. What that means is that I think and write like a dad and husband. What *that* means is that at least some of what I say and how I say it in this book might make a little less sense to anyone who isn't a dad and a husband. Along those same lines, some of what I think is really funny might seem to that same population like annoying dad humor that is only remotely entertaining if you find amusement in classic movies such as *Anchorman*, *The Big Lebowski*, or any movie starring Bill Murray. I'm okay with that if you are. The methodology of this book can work for the non-dads out there as well. It's just that if you are one of those non-dads, you might have to indulge me in some "Dadisms" along the way.

All of this brings me to a more serious and important point: I am not trying to "fix" the work world and change things that are out of my control at a broader macro level. As my dad used to tell me: "Fix what you can control. Don't worry about the rest." And so in this book, I have focused on solving the work-life balance problem by fixing what all of us can control at the individual level—our approach to work and life every day, our decisions around what to prioritize in work and life, and our willingness to accept hard trade-offs. Those were all things I needed to learn how to do better—for the sake of my family, my business, and my own mental and physical health. I hope the strategies and tactics (and my own story) revealed in this book help you with your own work-life balance challenges.

Getting Started:
What's Your Current State?

My approach to solving my work-life balance problem had started with a question that had me looking at the problem from a very different perspective—a business perspective. For my business clients who were initiating or even just thinking about transformation at any level, I frequently recommended starting with an important first step:

> *Assess your <u>current state</u>. Inventory what you are doing and not doing as things stand right now.*

For those business clients, a current state assessment served as an important baseline and helped identify the challenges that existed as things stood before transformation. Assessing the current state was often about documenting how work was currently getting done, who was doing that work, what initiatives were being worked on, and where the money was going. Before making any recommendations for them about what to do, we first needed to understand their current state. Then I could help them.

I clearly knew there was a problem with my work-life balance. Otherwise, I wouldn't have been asking my neighbor down the street for help to put an end to my naps on the travertine floor. What were the causes of those kitchen floor comas? I didn't know. I knew something was wrong, but I didn't have the detail to assess what was causing what and how to fix it. I had never taken the time to think about my current state in a way that would help me understand it. Who does? Most of our lives move fast. Some of you work for companies who operate at hyperspeed. Then you go home to fulfill dad responsibilities. Who has the time or energy to sit down and do a current-state self-analysis when your brain is still churning about your workday while you are trying to lead the post-dinner dog-pile game with your kids on the front lawn? By the time you do get a few free minutes, you have minimal energy to think and might just want to watch *SportsCenter* to escape into the latest Red Sox-Yankees drama. At least, that's the way it was for me.

Ironically, when I thought about my business clients, though, most of them were more than happy to get a current-state analysis as part of the work they hired me to do. It made the recommendations I would ultimately provide to them feel more meaningful and grounded in reality. Here's the bottom line. If you are looking to improve your work-life balance, why not start by doing a current-state assessment of your work and life? This assessment was my official first step in my journey towards work-life balance. It proved to be one of the most important things I did because it provided undeniable evidence with specificity and detail to help me see exactly where changes were needed. And as someone who works in the business world where metrics seem to follow you around wherever you go (including the bathroom), I could always go back to that current state as a qualitative baseline and compare it to the results from whatever changes I was making.

If you are wondering how to do a current-state analysis for your work and life, I recommend documenting a current day in your life as a way to see what is working and what isn't. This easy "day-in-the-life" exercise always works wonders with my clients, helping them see challenges in their business processes, investment priorities, culture, and operations that they were blind to for whatever reason. The information extracted from their day-in-the-life assessment often yielded realizations like: "I had no idea we were doing it that way." Sometimes, the information generated reactions like: "I thought we had stopped that process years ago. We are still doing that? Am I still paying for that?"

Until you do some version of the day-in-the-life approach, you can't know what traps you might be falling into again and again, hour by hour, that might be giving you no chance of finding your holy grail of work-life balance. And for many of us, the stress we feel around trying to achieve work-life balance comes in the minutes and hours every day, which a day-in-the-life helps deconstruct for you. It certainly did for me.

Doing an assessment like this might seem a bit a daunting at first, but it's a lot easier than you think. I didn't carry a secret notebook around with me all day to document every little thing that happened to me. Nor did I hire an expensive life coach to follow me around all day carrying his or her own secret notebook to document every little thing that happened to me. It will require only thirty minutes at the end of your day. Instead of watching *SportsCenter*, just write down how your day went, specifically what happened when and, maybe most importantly, how you were feeling as the day progressed during each of those key moments.

1. **When were your biggest stress points?**

2. **Why did those points feel the most stressful?**

3. **When were you feeling like you had control of what you were doing on both the work and life fronts?**

4. **When did you feel like you had little to no control?**

As you document your day, paint the picture of what really happened (the good, the bad, and the ugly); don't dilute or justify anything. We all put up a good front for everyone else. I did (and probably still do depending on the day). My standard answer when people asked me about work and life used to be: "Always busy but totally fun! I wouldn't do it any other way. Keeps life interesting and entertaining! Better busy than bored." Then I would walk away shaking my head, wondering who I needed to make a deal with for a few more minutes of boredom in my life. The good news is that your day-in-the-life isn't going to be published anywhere. You don't need to convince anyone (including yourself) that life is anything other than what it really is, so be completely honest as you paint your picture. I suspect if you are reading this book, you're looking for something to try a little differently anyway.

In the spirit of full transparency about my search for my own holy grail of work-life balance, I've chosen to show you a day in my life before things changed. It is a short chapter in this book. Your day-in-the-life assessment won't and shouldn't be this long. For explanatory purposes now and later in the book, I have chosen to describe events that happened in my day-in-the-life in more detail. You won't need to do that unless you plan on reading yours to a group of strangers at the open mic night at your local coffee shop. After reading my day-in-the-life, you might feel like yours is more severe or less acute. You also might conclude that I was a complete moron (about certain things), a bad parent (at times), and the luckiest businessperson alive who had no business still being in business. Any or all of those assessments might have been true. Maybe that's the real point here, though. When you don't have the balance you want at work or in your personal life, you aren't your best self in either place. You'll see that I wasn't. I'll come back to this day-in-the-life many times throughout the rest of the book. It shows lots of things I was doing wrong. It also shows the starting point in my search for work-life balance, my baseline from which I hoped to improve.

I have had lots of days that have looked and felt a lot like the one I'm about to share (minus some of the gory details). I hope that by reading about my day you might see how you are making some of these same mistakes—or even different ones—in your own quest for work-life balance. So go get a beer or whatever it is you drink at the end of the night. My beverage of choice is usually fat-free milk, but don't let that deter you from reading further.

A Day in the Life (in the Ludicrous Lane)

My day started out like most days seemed to start out—with me lying awake in bed at 4:30 in the morning. I didn't want to be awake at 4:30 in the morning. My eyes were heavy and barely open, and my alarm wasn't set to go off for another two hours. My brain had woken me up thinking about how many balls needed to be thrown in the air and miraculously caught over the next few days. I hadn't slept well. I was drained and hadn't even gotten out of bed yet. I coerced myself to get up, being careful to not wake my wife, Jen, or our three-month-old baby, Ivan, who was sleeping next to our bed in his bassinette. I stumbled in the dark over a baby toy left on the floor. As I recovered my balance and rubbed my eyes, I peeked into the bassinette, relieved to find Ivan still asleep. I looked over at my wife who was still sleeping. I saw her almost every day, but I missed her.

I inched out of our room, careful not to step on Jazzy, our dog, who was sleeping outside our door. She was snoring loudly enough that I worried that *she* was going to wake Ivan up. I crept down the stairs towards the first-floor bathroom like a burglar in my own house—clothes, toiletries, and cell phone in hand. I didn't bother turning the light on in the bathroom. I wasn't ready for the shock of light. I sat on the toilet in the dark and did what most working dads I knew did: I checked e-mail on my phone. I also checked my calendar and the long list of work and family to-dos for the day, which I noticed didn't seem to include eating. If recent history was a good predictor, at some point in the day I'd end up stuffing almonds into my mouth while driving with my cell phone on mute, listening to a conference call hoping I'd have enough time to swallow before needing to make a somewhat intelligent comment.

Today, my wife had the complicated task of juggling baby Ivan and Daniella—her twenty-year-old sister for whom we were legal guardians. Dani, who was a sophomore in college, was going through her early adulthood "finding herself" phase, which as recently as last week included acquiring a nose ring and a tattoo on her neck next to her ear that read: RESIST. Who was I to judge, though? Back in the day when I was trying to find myself, I had long hair, multiple piercings, and a self-appointed duty to party until I temporarily forgot where I lived.

I had our two-year-old son, Ben, for the morning, and I also had the other young adult member of our household—my wife's sixteen-year-old brother, Gabe, for whom we were also legal guardians. Sandwiched between and all around Teenager and Toddler Town was my job running my management consulting practice. I loved what I did and felt fortunate to be able to do it, but there was no mistaking the fact that it was a lot of work.

Work then life then back to work then back to life and back to work again. Back and forth all day long. I was about to enter the "Vortex"— my name for those days and weeks where everything seemed to collide, sucking me into a massive whirlwind. It was soccer and volleyball games, driving tests, and toddler speech therapy and swimming lessons having head-on collisions with leadership team meetings, big project milestones, and business writing deadlines. Didn't I just exit last week's Vortex? I rubbed my head and let out a long, audible breath. While still sitting on the toilet, I scanned my work e-mails, responding to the most urgent. They all felt urgent.

Forty-five minutes had passed quickly, and my legs were falling asleep. Numb legs happened most mornings and were my cue to stop the phone usage and move on. I stood up, turned the light on, brushed my teeth, and wiped the excess toothpaste from my face while putting my pants on. I noticed that I had grabbed one black sock and one blue sock in the dark upstairs. Damn. There was no way in hell I was going back upstairs and risk waking Ivan. I looked in the mirror. Dark circles under my eyes. At least my buzz-cut hair looked good, as it did every morning regardless of how tired I was; my choice of haircut strategically saved me five minutes of styling. As I hurried out of the bathroom, I heard scratching at the door to the garage. Ted, our pet rabbit, was letting me know that he wanted out from his safe nighttime sanctuary so that he could forage in our backyard. Tending to Ted's desires may not seem high on the priority list, but when Ted wasn't let out of the garage early in the morning, he had shown a propensity for finding the most important thing in there and chewing it until it became unrecognizable. I opened the garage door to see Ted staring up at me.

"What's up, Ted? Eat anything in there last night you want to tell me about?"

I had just asked a sarcastic question to a rabbit at 5:30 in the morning. My life was weird.

I went to the kitchen and shoved a banana in my mouth with one hand and packed Ben's bag for his morning activities with the other. He'd be up soon. I had to move quickly. As I cut up a peach and got oatmeal ready for his breakfast, I heard the usual morning sounds coming out of Ben's room. I finished throwing his stuff in his bag and headed upstairs. Outside his door, I heard him practicing his letters of the alphabet with great enthusiasm.

"Eeeeeeeeee! Ooooooooooh! Em em em em . . . Deeeeeeeeeeee!"

He was a cool little dude, and it was always fun to eavesdrop before going in. He had been diagnosed with a significant speech delay. We had him in physical therapy and speech therapy. He was trying really hard. So were we. His therapy was intensive, regular, and kind of expensive. But it's your kid so you do everything and anything that needs to be done, right? I opened the door to his room and poked my head in:

"Mama!!!" He pointed at the door towards our bedroom.

I changed his diaper, feeling a combination of relief and trepidation that we were going full steam ahead into potty training next week. Of course, still sitting untouched on my desk were the three potty training books Jen had asked me to read.

I brought Ben downstairs and turned on *Teletubbies*, which I had been adamantly against initially, given that I was convinced there was no way sober people made that show. After a few viewings, though, I changed my opinion. It was a weird show, but I interrogated a pet rabbit every morning. I was in no place to judge anyone else's weirdness. While Ben was eating, I triple checked his bag to make sure I had everything he needed. Gabe was up early as usual and watched *Teletubbies* with Ben, providing the usual teenage dystopian commentary to a two-year-old about how unrealistic the show was. I looked at the clock. We needed to get rolling.

7:30 a.m.: I started ushering Ben from the house to the car.

7:35 a.m.: I continued ushering Ben from the house to the car.

7:37 a.m.: I continued continuing to usher Ben from the house to the car.

7:38 a.m.: The distance between the front door and the car felt unattainable today.

7:40 a.m.: Almost had him in the car only for him to get distracted by the multicolored pinwheel on our front lawn.

7:42 a.m.: I redirected Ben with balls I had strategically left in his car seat. There you go.

As we drove off, I put the back-windshield wiper on so Ben could watch it. There was no rain. There were no clouds, but the distraction usually lasted just long enough to get to speech and physical therapy without him saying "Up!" every two seconds to signal his urgent desire to get out of the car. At the therapists' office, part of me wanted to stay out in the lobby to check my phone and work e-mails. Most of me wanted to be in there with Ben so I could see what they were doing and what we should be doing at home. I knew joining him was the right thing to do, but it also created a hovering cloud over my head that grew by the minute as I worried about e-mails I was getting behind on and work that needed immediate attention. Despite the cloud, I tried to focus on Ben's therapy. Embarrassingly, it was hard.

An hour later, therapy was done. Now we needed to get to swimming. It was 9:00, so we had thirty minutes to get there, and it was twenty minutes away. We didn't have any buffer since those last ten minutes were needed to get him changed and poolside. It was "just-in-time" scheduling. Of course, today, Ben was in slow-roll mode, wanting to play with every toy in the therapists' lobby, which was going to negatively impact the "in-time" part of that equation. I chose the carry-the-kid-like-a-football approach to end toy time. We were in the car and rolling, but we had lost five precious minutes.

9:15 a.m.: Orange cones and signs for road construction required a detour. I felt my pulse speed up a few ticks as I strongly considered testing my Subaru Outback's all-wheel drive over the chopped-up road. Instead, I clock watched.

9:23 a.m.: We made it to the YMCA. I jumped out of the car, got Ben out of his car seat, pulled his pants down, put his swim shorts on, and grabbed his swim bag in one fluid, effortless motion. (Not really. I bumbled through it.) I put Ben up on my shoulders and fast-walked into the pool. We made it with two minutes to spare.

As we walked towards the pool, I saw a mom whom I had seen many times at the YMCA. One of her sons was in Ben's class. She was a nice lady, had three young sons, and always seemed unsettlingly calm. She made managing kids look too easy. Her boys never had any shower tantrums, pool tantrums, or tantrums of any kind. I wondered if they had gotten some sort of vaccination for that.

With Ben now in the pool, I had a few minutes to relieve my growing angst about e-mail while making a quick bathroom pitstop. I opened up my e-mail on my phone while pit-stopping to save time. Surprised at how many e-mails had come in since my first check in the morning just a couple of hours earlier, I responded quickly to two of them, probably without as much thought or thumb dexterity as they needed. Almost immediately after I hit *SEND*, I noticed typos in one of them. I hated mistakes like that. I hurried back to the pool hoping I hadn't missed too much. Ben's teacher was walking him out of the pool. I looked around and noticed that all of the children were being walked out of the pool. Ben's teacher met me at the door.

"He pooped in the pool." No emotions on her face. No smile. No frown. No text-like emoticon. "See you next time." No emotion again. She then handed Ben off to me and walked away.

Oh f&#%! Ben looked up at me. He had an excited glimmer in his eyes and a big smile from ear to ear. I didn't. I had a big client meeting in a couple of hours, and my kid had just caused a mass pool evacuation at the local YMCA. For a minute, everything moved in slow motion. I vigorously rubbed my head a few times—a reflex habit of sorts. Did this just happen? Couldn't he have chosen another day? My mind oscillated back and forth between needing to solve a humongous poop issue right now and thinking about my hour commute rapidly approaching to get to the client meeting where no one would care about what my two-year-old had done in the pool today. I wondered what my wife would do. Then I wondered why I was wondering what my wife would do. There was no chance that I would triage this problem in a way that would even come close to being wife-sanctioned. This was going to get done dad style. My eyes darted to my watch again and then back at Ben. He was still standing there like a little happy frozen poop statue. It was time to get this thing done. I carried him from his armpits with his feet hanging in the air over to one of the private changing stalls as quickly as I could, being careful to cause as little "spillage" as possible. I saw Supermom out of the corner of my eyes in the shower with her boys. They were singing nursery rhymes and smiling. Of course they were.

Ben's swim diaper wasn't a pretty picture. This was a monster man-sized poop. For a second, I was strangely proud. In the stall, I took the nasty swim diaper off without causing too much attention directed our way. It wasn't a disposable swim diaper. I had a choice: Chuck it and call it a day? Or keep it and clean it? My dad gut said, "Chuck it," but my husband gut said, "Keep it and clean it, or you'll pay the price." Husband gut won.

I put the nasty swim diaper aside for now. Unfortunately, our scurrying to the stall had left a trail of wet poop on the floor. Embarrassing? Yes. Top priority right now? No. Supermom and her kids were too busy being perfect to notice anyway. I ushered now naked but still smiling Ben over to the shower while holding my hand behind his shoulders to keep him from deviating from our direct line to the showers. Usually, getting Ben into the shower was a challenge that required lots of "influencing skills," in other words, goldfish crackers. Today for some reason, he put up no resistance.

"Thank you, Ben! You are doing a great job!" I said with hyped-up repetition.

We had a remote shower stall so there weren't too many other parents around to watch this dad-style cleanup. We did a fast wash. No teaching moments for Ben to get better at showering himself. Dad did all the work to get this done quickly. With Ben clean, I looked around at the fallout from this poop nuclear explosion. Ben was totally naked, and I could tell that he was itching to start running around the YMCA. Right now, I didn't care. He was two. It wasn't like *I* was running around the YMCA naked. Time to clean up all signs of the poop bombing. I yanked out two handfuls of paper towels from the dispenser to clean up the poop trail. Chucked them in the trash can. One of the YMCA guys started mopping up the floor after me. He said nothing to me. I said nothing to him. We made slight eye contact. Maybe we'd talk about this later. Maybe we wouldn't. Maybe he was a dad, too, and, in dad solidarity, was assisting with the cleanup, helping to cover up any evidence that a "situation" had occurred here at all.

I surveyed the area. Area cleaned. Check. Ben clean. Check. Still naked. Whatever. Now for the disastrous swim diaper. I had to get that gnarly thing to a sink where I could rinse it with hot water, wring it out, wash it, and get it back to some semblance of what it was before Ben had bombed it. All of this had to be done before the very short-lived self-restraining system in my naked two-year-old's brain gave in and let him run amok. The locker room where I had checked my e-mails was right next to the showers. If I got Ben in there with me, he could be contained while I washed the gnarly diaper.

"Hey, Ben, let's get some fruit snacks! I've got yellow and orange. Your favorites!"

Sure, the dentist had told us to use those fruit snacks sparingly because they were bad for his teeth. I'll admit this was not my finest moment in toddler-influencing tactics. I wasn't feeling like "Dad of the Year." But we were in a state of emergency. Let the fruit snacks roll. The dentist wasn't here. And these were just baby teeth anyway. The lure worked easily. I, of course, grabbed a few for myself . . . you know, to test them. Man, those things were good. I hoped I had another bag in the car. For Ben. Yeah, for Ben. Fortunately, no one else was in the locker room. I jiggled the lock to try to lock the door. The lock jiggled. The lock didn't lock. We'd just have to take the risk that Ben would escape or someone would come in and see us fully engulfed in this poop mess. Or both. I put Ben in there, ran out to collect his swim stuff, including the swim diaper, and brought everything into the locker room. I wiped my forehead. *Was it hot in here?* Ben followed me over to the sink. I turned on the hot water and dropped the diaper in the sink. Wow, this thing was nasty at a legendary level. I wrung it out over and over. Ben stood there like a compliant little dude. I couldn't have been prouder of him. Then I looked over at the locker room door and saw another trail of poop, from the door to the sink. This thing was like the movie *The Blob*. It had a life of its own. Solve one thing. Then there's another. It felt remarkably like what I did at work every day. I smirked.

I stuck my hand under the electronic paper towel dispenser; a paper towel shot out. I had *Matrix*-speed hand movements, and I did this with rapid fire until I had about ten paper towels. I was about to clean up the poop trail when something unexpected happened. Ben was standing next to me, looking up and laughing hysterically. I stopped and looked at him. The urgency of the moment suddenly evaporated, and time stopped for a second. A big smile came over my face when I realized that Ben had never seen an electronic paper towel dispenser. He thought it was the funniest thing he had ever seen. Every time I stuck my hand under the dispenser, he would laugh harder. Ben was having a great time. Maybe that was all that mattered. He wasn't emotionally scarred by this incident and didn't have any idea that he had caused the pool to be closed for the rest of the day for detoxification. He just thought this hand-waving, paper-towel-dispensing thing Daddy was doing was funny as hell.

With Ben laughing in the background and clamoring for MORE! I cleaned up the final poop trail. I washed my hands three times and spent the next five minutes unnecessarily dispensing a huge amount of paper towels just to make my son laugh. I wasn't going to get an invitation to the local chapter of "Dads for a Greener Planet," but I figured Earth would forgive me for a brief environmental lapse because my kid thought this was the best moment of his life. Ben and I laughed together for the next five minutes. It was just as funny the seventeenth time as it was the first. We walked out of the locker room. Ben and I had survived "Poopgate." As I frequently told my wife about how things went when I was on kid duty: *We win ugly, but we win.*

I let out a deep breath and suddenly felt winded. My Poopgate adrenaline was wearing off. There was no time to relax, though. We had to get a move on because I still had that big client meeting to get to, as well as a pile of other work to do. I was now very behind and felt my pulse racing. As we rushed back to the car, Supermom was getting her three boys into their car. I expected to see the boys magically floating into their seats unassisted. But then:

"Watch the door, Brady! You can't just swing the door open! You hit that car! Get in the car!" Brady was the older boy squirming around like a snake, and the younger boys were both crying but with slightly different pitches just to make the combined effort that much more irritating.

"Oh yeah!" I said too audibly. Then I felt guilty about reveling in the fact that for one brief moment the playing field had been leveled between Supermom and a dad who wins ugly.

We arrived home around 11:25 a.m. I ran around the car, grabbed Ben, and lifted him out of the car. I opened the front door to the house, and our neurotic dog—filled with pent-up energy—bolted out and whacked Ben in the head with her tail. He cried. I couldn't have more delays right now. I ran to the kitchen cabinet and grabbed a piece of fig bar to give him as a distraction. If I was going to have a bad snack-dispensing day, why not go all the way? Tomorrow, I'd feed him broccoli all day long.

I hurried inside with Ben, sat him in his high chair, gave him his lunch, ran to the backyard to corral our eight chickens back into their coop, ran back out to the front yard to the car, emptied it as quickly as I could, put the now infamous swim diaper in a plastic bowl with soap to soak, ran back inside forgetting to close the back car door, ran upstairs skipping two steps at a time, pulled on my work clothes, left my shirt untucked until later, and ran back downstairs. I grabbed my computer bag, gave a hasty wave to my wife and Ivan—who had just come through the front door—and said something to my wife that sounded more like caveman talk than anything else:

"Ben. Poop. Pool. Talk later . . ."

She looked confused. I rushed out to the car and was on the road by noon. On a good day without any unforeseen traffic issues, my drive to the client was an hour. Today, best case, I'd arrive fifteen minutes before the meeting started—not nearly enough time to get everything set up the right way. As I drove, I did guerilla prep for the meeting. I was really hungry. I found almonds on the backseat. My morning lunch prediction turned out to be accurate.

Three-quarters of the way there, a sea of red brake lights emerged in front of me and went on for as far as I could see. I hit the steering wheel and groaned as I looked at the clock: 12:42. Now I worried that I was actually going to be late. I glanced outside the passenger-side window and noticed a runner on the road parallel to the freeway. He ran past me. I clenched the steering wheel and fidgeted in my seat as we crawled along. The phone rang. It was a potential client. I wanted the work, even though I was already slammed with client work and struggling to get it all done without damaging current client relationships or shortchanging my family. Still, I never turned down an opportunity. Maybe it was fear that another one wouldn't materialize. Maybe it was the fact that I was the sole financial provider for my family. Maybe it was the lingering advice of my late dad, who, as my greatest mentor, had always told me to take advantage of every opportunity you get. I took the call. While talking, my phone beeped; today's client texted: YOU ALMOST HERE?

Miraculously out of nowhere, the brake lights went off, and the road opened up. I slammed the gas and accelerated back up to seventy miles per hour, ripping past that runner. My phone beeped again as new texts came through. I tried to read them through the corner of my eye as I exited the freeway, taking the loop too fast and causing my can of almonds to slide across the front seat onto the floor. One text was from my mom: CAN WE COME SEE THE BOYS SOON? NEED SOME GRANDSON TIME. The text was followed by seven emojis, three of which I understood. Another was a work text about a new project: BELL PROJECT STARTS NEXT WEEK. LET'S TALK ABOUT KICKOFF DETAILS. I couldn't respond now. Within ten minutes, I arrived at the client site, grabbed my computer bag, threw open the car door, stood up and tucked in my shirt in the parking lot, hurried into the building, texted my client: I'M HERE, and entered the conference room. I wiped my forehead. *Was it hot in here?*

It was 1:20, five minutes past our scheduled start time. I wasn't going to say anything if they weren't. Then I learned that one team member was running about twenty minutes late, and we needed to wait to start until she arrived. I had promised Gabe that I would attend his club volleyball game after work. Starting twenty minutes late was going to put that in jeopardy. How was I going to pull this off? I had twenty-five minutes to think about it because we didn't officially start until 1:45.

After several hours, we managed to close the meeting at 5:20, a little later than expected, but I still had a chance to make Gabe's 6:00 game. I shook everyone's hands after a successful meeting and walked out the door; my walk turned to a jog as soon as my client couldn't see me anymore. I was now almost a half hour late. I felt winded again. Got in the car and sent a text to Gabe: JUST GETTING OUT OF THE CLIENT NOW. HEADING OVER TO YOUR GAME. HOPING TO BE THERE BY 6. I then screamed out of the parking lot, went out the wrong exit, and drove around in a circle to get back on the right street. *Damnit.* I approached the freeway a few minutes later and looked out at a sea of cars. It was the usual rush hour crawl. A guttural sound of hostility came out of my throat—a sound I wasn't sure how I had even made. Jazzy would have been impressed. *Damnit.* But it was rush hour every day at 5:30. This wasn't a new development.

After merging into the crawl, I called my mom back. When it came to the grandkids, if I waited too long to call her back, she was known to jump to worst-case scenarios that usually involved rare illnesses. She was a Jewish grandmother. It was her job to worry about things at an exaggerated level. She did her job well. I then checked my voice mail. Seven new messages had come through while I was in the working session—four client calls, an annoying computer-to-voice-mail message, someone looking for someone named Lucy, and my dentist reminding me of an appointment on Wednesday. *Damn*. I had forgotten about that. I had postponed three dentist appointments in a row, at the very last minute each time. Were they going to fire me as a patient? Could they?

I had to find time to return these calls at some point tomorrow. Then I realized that I hadn't checked e-mail since 11:30 a.m., which violated my self-imposed e-mail checking code of conduct that required me to obsessively check e-mail any time I wasn't doing anything else.

5:40 p.m.: I thought about trying to log into my e-mail account while driving. I didn't.

5:42 p.m.: Again thought about trying to log into my e-mail while driving. Again didn't.

5:44 p.m.: Looked over at my phone again thinking I could check my e-mail if I got lucky enough to hit more traffic. *Really?*

At a little after six, I arrived at the high school where Gabe's game was taking place. Somehow, I was only five minutes late for game time. I ran to the gym. I was surprised to see the team still warming up. I offered a confused hello to one of the dads I knew and found out the game actually started at 6:45. I had made it on time but only because my head was so cluttered that I had the game time wrong. At least I wouldn't miss it. I sat in the stands and opened up my e-mail on my phone. Then I saw the football stadium was right outside and realized that I could get a mini work-out in. *Screw the e-mail.*

I ran back out to the car, reached into the backseat, and pulled out my shorts and running shoes that I always kept back there. At least the clothes were there, even if they'd been there untouched for a while. I changed as stealthily as I could in the front seat of the car to avoid any risk of being charged with indecent exposure. I needed some exercise, and exercise never seemed to be on the high priority list anymore, despite years of it being first on the list. How life had changed. I set the timer on my cell phone and ran up and down the stairs of the stadium.

The alarm went off ten minutes before game time. I stopped mid staircase, got some water, and ran back inside. Concerned about my sweat and the general heat now radiating from my body, I sat far away from the other parents, hoping they didn't think I was being antisocial. The game hadn't started yet. I could have relaxed for a few minutes. Instead, I checked my e-mail again. I was feeling the pressure of whatever was in my inbox that I had been blind to since before lunch. My head was buried in my phone before I realized that the game had already started. I pulled myself out of it, sat back, and tried to enjoy watching the game. My body was still tense. The lingering effects from running around all day had me tired. I couldn't clear my head. I was physically there at the game, but I was mentally somewhere else for parts of it. Gabe's team won in straight sets, as usual. They were good.

I hurried down the stands and talked briefly with Gabe and a few of his teammates. Gabe had played very well. The team played very well. Gabe had some good friends on the team. I enjoyed watching them win and have fun together. It was nice to be there for Gabe, even though most of his attention these days was with his friends. Staying connected with Gabe was a high priority of mine. He was poised to finish high school strong and head off to college. Gabe and another teammate got their things together at "teenage speed" (a pace very similar to the slow-rolling toddler speed I had experienced with Ben earlier), and we headed out to the car. I was on carpool duty for transport home from today's game. Sometimes, I felt like a shuttle service that made no money. At least on the car ride home, I was able to use the time with Gabe as a captive audience to remind him to sign up for the SAT prep class we had been talking about. My stomach growled as we drove home. As hungry as I was, I wanted to see Ben and Ivan before they went to bed.

After dropping off Gabe's friend at his house, we drove straight home. I walked in the door at about 7:30 p.m. As he often did when I came home, Ben ran around the corner to the door screaming with excitement:

"Dada!! Dada!! Dada!!"

"Hey, Big Ben! Want to read some books with Daddy?"

Ben's exuberance gave me the temporary energy boost I needed. I was tired, but reading books with the little dude was an awesome experience. One day, he'd probably complain about reading and certainly wouldn't want to read with me. These times were sacred and would be short-lived. I knew that. After about fifteen minutes, it was time to take Ben up to bed. I was hoping this wouldn't require any more dad "influencing" tools because they were all used up today. And giving fruit snacks to a kid you are trying to get to sleep is something even I knew not to do.

Okay, Ben was down. I was tired as hell and starving. I headed downstairs and grabbed some leftover food from the day before. My wife looked over at me while sitting on the couch feeding Ivan. He was awesome—all eighteen pounds of him, a really big guy for only three months old. I sat at the table in the dark eating. A few minutes later, I held Ivan so Jen could eat her dinner. We played around as he gave me massive toothless gum smiles. It didn't take long for Ivan to start to fall asleep. My wife took him from me and put him to bed in his bassinette in our room. He'd most likely sleep through the night. Thank god. Gabe was now sequestered up in his room binge watching *The Office* and gaming. Hopefully, we'd be spared any late-night teenage drama tonight. I gave us a 50 percent chance at best. I still had work to do. Around 9:30, I reluctantly took out my laptop to finish some client work. The notion of working that late made me a little grumpy, but I had two PowerPoint presentations to finish. I sat at the kitchen table, with bad posture and insufficient light, and worked quietly.

An hour later, I closed my laptop and rubbed my eyes. My head was feeling clogged. I wasn't sick. It always felt like this by the end of the day. I slowly walked up the stairs to take a shower. I thought about the long list of e-mails I still needed to get to and the work-related things I had hoped to get done today that just didn't materialize. I brushed my teeth with my eyes closed and got in the shower. Afterwards, I walked quietly across the hall to check on Ben and adjust his blanket. Ben needed his blanket adjusted every night, but my going in there was mostly an excuse to take a moment of silence to watch him. If that didn't confirm what was really important, nothing would.

I walked back across the hall to our room and sat on the edge of our bed. By now, it was after eleven. I thought for a second about checking e-mail before bed and quickly decided against it. I opened my phone to my to-do list and transferred to tomorrow seven things I was sure I would have gotten done today. This transfer seemed to happen every night and had been happening for as long as I could remember. I then pulled up my calendar to check tomorrow's schedule. It was going to be as full as today, more so now that I had transferred over today's uncompleted tasks. The spillover effect had already started, and it was only Monday. I looked at tomorrow's list. I had to:

1. Read potty training books for Ben. (I was now highly motivated.)

2. Catch up on the twenty-five work e-mails I had passed on tonight.

3. Prepare for my 8:00 a.m. client call.

4. Finalize and send in the business article I had written.

5. Update my revenue tracking system with paid invoices and projected revenue.

6. Figure out the timing of my IRS payment for a tax contribution to the business.

7. Take Ben to his new speech therapy evaluation center. (We had been working for weeks to get him into a clinic that better fit his needs. This was nonnegotiable.)

8. Reschedule a client lunch to a client call so that I could get #7 done.

9. Draft a business transformation strategy for another client.

10. Prepare for four executive coaching sessions next week.

11. Return calls to the four clients who had left voice mails earlier.

12. Prepare for my upcoming business trip to Texas later in the week.

13. Call the insurance company and add Ivan to our health insurance.

14. Pay bills.

15. Do a radio interview for the book I had recently published.

16. Take Ben out for his afternoon neighborhood walk for a couple of hours to prevent him from turning the house upside down in the late afternoon.

17. Go to the bank to make a few adjustments to my business account.

18. Prepare for a session I was teaching at a client next week.

11:25 p.m.: Got into bed.

11:26 p.m.: Passed out.

Part II: The Work-Life Equation.
No Calculus Required.

Deconstructing a Day in Your Life

Well, there it is. That was a day in my life. That was life as I knew it before I started making changes. Was it a typical day for me? With the exception of my kid pooping in the community pool, it was more typical than I would have hoped. Your day-in-the-life analysis will have its own unique elements. Some of you may find that you are bouncing around between work and life just like I was. Some of you may find that you can't get to as much life stuff as you want to because your day is slammed with work. That's a scenario I typically hear. There are lots of versions of this. The thing they all have in common is that the day doesn't feel balanced in a way that brings enjoyment and satisfaction.

Once you've assessed your day, you need to do something with that information. What did *I* do next? Other than moving my drink of choice from fat-free milk to a cold beer (for that day, at least), I did what I do with my business clients. After I have documented a day-in-the-life scenario for them, my first step is to deconstruct it into some key observations at a glance. What are the major themes that jump out? What are the key trends? What behaviors or situations keep surfacing? For my clients, it is also about noting things that were happening that they may not have even realized were happening. All of these questions are important to ask when deconstructing your own day-in-the-life.

Sometimes, it may be helpful to have someone else review your day-in-the-life and tell you what they see. This works for the same reason that my business clients often aren't able to see some things they are doing every day. They are simply too close to the day-to-day operations of their business to raise up a bit and look down on their own fish bowl (and do so objectively and without judgement or justification). Once I had finished documenting my day-in-the-life, I let my wife take a look at it, despite the fact that I was giving her a window into her husband's never-before-revealed poop triage approach, which might validate her suspicion that her husband had no parenting common sense whatsoever. I took the risk and am still happily married.

In simple terms, the key here is to figure out three or four major takeaways from your day-in-the-life that can give you some direction. For me, my day-in-the-life highlighted what I now describe as my well-intentioned but misguided work-life circus clown juggling. I made four key observations (which were all conveniently validated by my wife):

1. I had a really long list of things I was trying to get done in a day, and that overstacked list created stress.

2. I had no wiggle room in my day for anything to go wrong. That created stress because it didn't take much to knock me completely off schedule.

3. I was bouncing back and forth between work and life all day long. Being a human pinball created stress because my mind could never get into a comfort zone.

4. I had no plan. I had a list of things to do, but that wasn't really a plan for how I was managing work-life balance. This observation was somewhat ironic because my wife said I was a compulsive planner who planned how he was going to plan, to which I responded that I can be as spontaneous as the next guy if you just give me a little time to prepare to be spontaneous. But I had to face the fact that I really had no work-life balance plan. That might have been the biggest observation I was able to get out of my day-in-the-life.

You will have your own key observations. Some of your observations may look a lot like mine. Some won't. The point of the day-in-the-life exercise, though, is forced reflection for those of us who usually don't have any time for reflection. As I continued with my own reflection, I made a few additional observations: Everything always seemed to get done. Work was going well; my business was flourishing, and I was proud of that. I wasn't an absentee dad or husband. I was present and did lots of things with the family. But I often wasn't enjoying what I was doing, even though everything on the list was getting done. I was overwhelmed and feeling like I was running at hyperspeed all day long every day with no rest for the weary. There are unwritten and unspoken dad rules, and as far as I understand them, one is that you aren't allowed to admit that you are feeling overwhelmed. Admitting being overwhelmed violates the dad code I had been raised with: dads can handle anything and everything. I kept a lid on my stress and pushed through it all. But I wasn't taking care of myself, physically and emotionally, at all. I certainly was an absentee friend, too, and I couldn't remember the last time my wife and I had done something just for ourselves.

What my day-in-the-life triggered was the realization that maybe I was more responsible for my own work-life challenges than I thought. And that's really what the rest of this book is about for all of us—taking a hard look at how you manage your day and the impact it has on how balanced you feel (or don't feel). For me, I clearly needed to take a hard look at how I was living, or I might collapse one day. I didn't want my tombstone to say something like:

Here lies James Sudakow. He died trying to get it all done. At least he had enough sense to take out that nice life insurance policy.

So where do you go from here? Once you have your observations from your day-in-the-life, it is time to take action and do something with those observations. You could just jump in and start solving the key problems as identified in your observations. However, as I've learned in working with my business clients, if you solve problems without first developing a clear vision of your desired future state, your solutions may not align with where you ultimately want to be. The day-in-the-life represents your current state, but you also need to figure out your hoped-for future state in order to take action appropriately. That's the next step in the process I followed. So put the current state aside for a minute. We'll come back to it in spades.

Now you need to do some future visioning, which will require some serious thinking. When I did this, I drove to the local library down the street—which had become my de facto "office" over the last few months—since at home, taking my laptop into the bathroom to get work done uninterrupted and taking conference calls in my bedroom closet to avoid the noise of kids, dog, and chickens was a comically ineffective approach to running a business or contemplating my work-life balance situation. For you, just go wherever you can get a little uninterrupted thinking time.

If You Don't Define It, You'll Never Get It

Without knowing the balance you want, you can't get the balance you want.

My day-in-the-life had shown me a lot of things. One of the most important was that I had no plan for my work-life balance. In fact, most people I've talked to haven't really thought about a formal work-life balance plan or strategy. Some of us have bucket lists. We have long lists of things to get done every day. But neither of those represent a plan or a strategy for work-life balance. So how do you come up with one?

To solve this, I went back to the work I do with some of my clients. Sometimes companies hire me to help with business transformation. A lot changes in the business world, and these days it seems to change faster than ever. Because of that, many companies are trying to figure out how they need to change to stay competitive, or even just survive. That often means determining their vision, or defining their North Star, so that they can steer the business towards it as they transform. Without a clearly defined vision, it would be like they were trying to guide a ship in the middle of the ocean with no navigation. I spend a lot of time with clients defining that business vision with as much clarity as we can.

Our searches for work-life balance shouldn't be any different. I knew that I wanted to be successful in my business and be an active part of my family—the usual line that a lot of us probably use. However, if I went one level beneath that line, it didn't really mean anything. It was a sound bite so generic that everything or nothing could fit into it. A sound bite wouldn't help me figure out what really mattered to me, and if you are using the same party line, it might not help you. Maybe more importantly, it couldn't explain what a balanced day should look like. And the day level is where work-life balance happens for most of us—or doesn't happen. It is in the minutes and hours of every day that stress builds from trying to do this specific thing or that explicit activity. Generic sound bites don't help you reconcile any of that. The bottom line is that if you talk only in general terms, you really can't put specific strategies in place to help you achieve whatever it is that you want.

Assessing what is important to you at this point in time—and making trade-offs

To find your North Star, you need to get into detail about what *exactly* work-life balance looks like for you and what *specific* trade-offs you need to make to get there. My personalized work-life balance vision needed something more explicit than: "I want to run a successful business and be an active part of the family." As I thought about that next level of detail, I realized that I had no idea what to say beyond that generic statement. As much as I had made every effort to attain balance for the last decade of parenthood, I never knew what I really wanted at any point in those ten years. I had been shooting in the dark. No wonder my search for the holy grail of work-life balance had felt more like a series of comical calamities worthier of a Monty Python movie than a meaningful search for real and attainable work-life happiness. I was letting it all happen *to* me based on a nice-sounding but in the end useless view of balance.

How then do you get to something meaningful and useful? I started by doing something that comes quite naturally to me in situations like this. I overanalyzed it. From time to time, the world needs to be overanalyzed—or at least our lives need to be overanalyzed. I had clearly been underanalyzing mine for years, so why not swing the pendulum the other way. The result couldn't be any worse than swirling around in my Vortex with eight chickens and a garage-eating rabbit for the rest of my life.

After thinking hard while staring into space for a very long time and probably leaving a new permanent wrinkle on my forehead, I wrote down three questions that kept circling around in my head. These three questions became the basis for determining a work-life balance vision:

1. **At this specific point in your life, are you someone who lives to work or works to live?** This is about forcing yourself to identify where your priorities stand. Given your life at the current moment, are you in the work camp or the life camp? Each represents priorities. Life clearly isn't this black and white, but it is important to remove the convenient answer of "both" that many of us are inclined to use. For thinking purposes, it becomes important to force yourself to pick a side.

2. **What are you not willing to give up on the work front?** This is about understanding what you perceive as nonnegotiable at work. You need to know what you aren't willing to compromise at work in the name of things you want in your personal life, regardless of how you answered the first question.

3. **What are you not willing to give up on the life front?** This is about doing the same thing as the second question but identifying the deal breakers in your personal life that you aren't willing to give up in the name of things you want from work.

There are no right or wrong answers to any of the three questions. As I was thinking about these questions for myself, I had an important realization. It would be very easy to answer these questions the way I thought I was supposed to answer them (you know, to be "socially acceptable") instead of being really honest with myself. But by being brutally honest, as a starting point, your answers will more accurately inform where your heart and mind are, where your priorities need to be, and maybe most importantly what trade-offs you are willing to accept to achieve those work-life balance priorities.

Of course, I soon realized that these questions were harder to answer than I originally anticipated. Now I knew why I had kept this work-life balance idea to a generic sound bite and why the holy grail of work-life balance had been so elusive. Who knew that three seemingly straightforward questions could be this difficult to answer? The questions forced me to consider trade-offs I had never thought about before. After a few headaches and some hard thinking, I wrote down some answers. I felt a little flashback to grade school when I turned in a test where I wasn't sure of the answers. I'm showing you my answers so you can get a sense for how I approached these questions as you think about them for yourself:

1. **At this specific point in your life, are you someone who lives to work or works to live?**

   Works to live.

2. **What are you <u>not</u> willing to give up on the work front?**

Being in business for myself. Doing whatever it takes to keep my business going. Keeping the pipeline of work filled to current levels to ensure business sustainability for the long term since I am the sole financial provider for the family. I don't want to work for a company that isn't my own right now.

3. What are you **not** willing to give up on the life front?

Spending quality time every week with Ivan. Spending quality time every week with Ben. Spending quality time every week with Jen. Being an active part of Gabe's life in high school and helping him along the path to success in college. Being there to support Dani on whatever she needs as she goes through college and beyond. I am not willing to outsource the raising of my kids in the name of running my business. Being a support for my mom and sister after my dad's passing. My health. Traveling to a few places my wife and I have always wanted to go: Iceland, Patagonia, Peru, the Galapagos, and Madagascar. Some form of regular contact with my lifelong friends.

When I looked at my answers, three distinct components of work-life balance emerged that needed to be incorporated into my work-life vision. Two were obvious, but the third was something I hadn't thought about before asking myself these questions.

1. **Work:** For me, this was about running my business in a sustainable way and everything that was part of that. Before I had my own business, when we were raising only Dani and Gabe, this was about excelling at my job in another company so that I was well regarded and in good stead at the company. Ultimately, though, what it was really about in either case was bringing home a specific amount of money to pay for everything else in our complicated house and beyond. I was the sole financial provider. For you, this category is about whatever you are doing and want out of your work.

1. **Life:** In the way I looked at it, life was everything not work but not about me individually.

1. **Me:** When I did my life list the first time, I was noticeably missing. That might have been a result of my place in life with two young children, a teenager, and a young adult, not to mention my sister and mom who were still adapting to life after my dad passed away

a year and a half ago. These days, life was about taking care of others. If you are a dad, you might be in a similar position, whether you have young kids or older kids. Regardless of your situation, *you* are an important part of the work-life balance equation. In pre-dad days, life was probably less complex, at least as it related to kids running around requiring your attention. So it was probably easier to make sure you were in the work-life equation. Not now. As you try to fulfill your dad obligation of making sure everyone is taken care of, you shouldn't push your own needs aside. Some of you might inherently be better at this than I was. Some of you might be worse at it.

With the three components of work-life balance clarified, I went back and looked at my answers. I noticed that I had a lot of nonnegotiables on the life side. As you look at your answers, you may have more on one side or the other. It doesn't matter which side your specific nonnegotiables are weighted towards. What does matter is how much time those priorities take. After all, we are all confined to twenty-four hours in a day and seven days in a week. So how was I going to do all of my life nonnegotiables while still running, building, and growing my business? Servicing clients, creating a pipeline for new business, overseeing projects and people, managing the day-to-day operations, writing for business publications, and everything else that was required to run the business wasn't going to happen on only twenty hours a week. My first pass at these answers had given me a road to walk on—which was more than my original sound bite—but I needed more information before the answers would be meaningful in a way that I could take action.

As you think about your answers to the three questions, you may need to dig deeper into your aspirations for work, life, and self. I did; it was the only way to get at the critical question of time. In other words, how are you going to parcel out your daily allotted twenty-four hours now that you have a view of what you'd like your priorities to be? In companies, having a great vision that has too much to it ultimately burns out the employees responsible for doing the work required to achieve that vision. The same thing could very easily happen with an unattainable work-life vision. Answering the finite time question is critical to making sure you are biting off exactly what you can chew. To get there, I went deep and asked some follow-up questions based on my answers to the initial three questions. Unfortunately, I can't create those follow-up questions for you, but it is an important step in the process. Your specific follow-up questions will inevitably be different than mine because they will be based on your personal answers to the first three questions. Here were mine:

1. **Since I said that "quality time" with my kids was important, what are my highest priorities for achieving that quality time every week?**

   Big Ben: Take and pick him up from preschool on his designated days, do one full-day weekend outing with him every weekend, take him to speech/physical therapy each week to be part of his development, do an afternoon activity with him at least two days a week, read to him at night at least four days a week. Be present enough to play an active role in shaping his values and behaviors.

   Ivan The Tank: Play with him every day, read to him at night with Big Ben, and evolve into the same things I do with Ben as Ivan gets older. Once he is done nursing, my role is going to ramp up a lot. I need time in the day for that.

   Gabe: Attend 75 percent of his soccer and volleyball games, work with him to prepare his college applications, take him on college tours, help him navigate the drama of high school, keep him focused on the most important things at a time when the most important things to a teenager might not be the most important things.

   Dani: Simply be available to support her whenever she wants my support.

2. **Since I had said that I wanted to spend quality time with my wife each week, what specifically do I want to do that would make me feel like we had achieved quality time together?**

   Dinner or lunch once a week just to ourselves. (That didn't seem like much, but it had been hard to make happen recently.)

3. **What specifically do I need to do each week to ensure my health?**

Thirty minutes at the gym three times a week and some time every day for James-zone-out-nobody-is-in-my-face time.

4. What specifically do I need to do to support my mom and sister?

Get Big Ben and Ivan the Tank over to Grandma's and Aunt Sarah's house every other week.

5. What specifically do I need to do every week to keep some form of contact with my lifelong friends?

Call, text, and e-mail my friends each week even if we can't hang out much anymore. Find time once every few months to at least try to get together in person. (I had been notably horrific at doing this for quite some time and was simply thankful that my friends still called me a friend.)

6. What do I need to do every week to successfully run my business while taking into consideration everything else I had already identified as important?

This was the hardest question to answer. What did running a successful business mean? Did it mean growing the business a certain percent every year? Did it mean blowing the doors off? Did it mean keeping revenues exactly where they were? Or did it mean undertaking something that had always been unspeakable— shrinking the business so that I could allocate more time to those life priorities I had just written down? I had never contemplated any of those questions before. Even before starting my business, I had never considered the notion of anything other than career growth—ascending versus staying in place. Neither was wrong or right, just like neither growing or shrinking a business was wrong or right. The question was how those work decisions fit with the overall vision I wanted for work and life *together, at my current place in life.* And for where I was in life now, the previously unspeakable idea of reducing business growth might need to be spoken. Maybe I didn't need to have the biggest business I could build. Instead, maybe I needed the right-sized business to enable work-life balance and to keep the family ship from sinking for lack of enough money coming in the door. I took a shot at writing down what running a successful business might mean in terms of day-to-day business activity:

*Keep my current clients, do quality and timely work for them, and identify new work that makes sense for their business. Stay ahead of things and identify where current clients may begin to erode. Actively engage with my business network to identify new opportunities for work to supplement any potential revenue degradation. **Define my bottom-end income threshold** (in other words, that revenue level that I can't allow my business to fall below) and monitor attainment of it. Say "no" or "not now" to new client opportunities that stretch beyond keeping the business in sustainability mode and put me back into growth mode. Minimize unnecessary business and financial expenses since I'm not growing the business right now. Continue writing weekly articles for business journals to keep my business reputation intact.*

Now I felt like I was getting somewhere. I had forced myself to be honest and specific about what I wanted and what I was and wasn't willing to give up to achieve my desired work-life balance. From doing this, I had more clarity on both the work and life fronts than I had ever had. Documenting this level of specificity may seem like an onerous task. Doing so will give you a sense of clarity that you probably didn't have before, though, which can bring peace of mind instead of the anxiety that comes from just winging it. Once you've got your priorities outlined, though, the work isn't done. Now you have to make sure that all of this is really doable.

Is there a such thing as "work-life balance math"?

As I worked through this approach, I took my overanalysis to another level of overanalysis. How many hours in a day or a week would it take to do all of these priorities? Were there going to be enough hours to pull it all off? This ultimately becomes the most important question because it determines whether your list is actually doable or whether you need to tighten that list up. Given the lack of precision inherent in estimating time requirements for certain work and life priorities, this might seem like dangerous overanalysis territory—the kind of overanalysis that had me worried I'd be left sitting in a catatonic state in the garage watching reruns of *Curious George* for some prolonged period of time, only to wake up and find that Ben was now a sophomore in high school. The

challenge is making the math work. How many hours will your list add up to? Here's how I approached figuring that out.

I went back to each of the priorities. In the "life" areas, my priorities for Ben, Ivan, Dani, and Gabe hadn't changed much from before my visioning exercise, but at least I now had them written down. I had added some priorities for my wife and friends, and I had made an attempt to significantly change my priorities for my business. Going from high growth to sustainability or even slight reduction mode was a notable change in focus.

Some of my priorities on the work and life fronts were easy to ascribe an estimated number of hours required. I knew how long swimming lessons took and how long it took to give a toddler a shower after the swimming lessons—although shower time certainly depended on Ben's mood and whether I remembered the goldfish crackers. At least there was some sort of baseline I could put on paper. I also had a pretty good sense for how long most of my business activities took. Not only had I been running this business for eight years, but I had been doing this kind of work throughout my career, even when I worked in various roles for other people in other companies. I simply mapped those hours as a starting point. Because of my experience, I made good momentum on the business side to get some real clarity around time spent and on what.

Figuring out the number of hours needed for work was far easier than the time needed for life. I probably shouldn't have been surprised about that; the dad section of my brain still needed some work. I had been in my career a lot longer than I had been a dad. Some of those personal priorities were a nightmare to figure out. How do you calculate what's required to keep a teenager on the right path? How do you calculate how much time is required to be present at home as an equal partner with my wife in dealing with toddler and teenage issues and associated drama? How do you even quantify the unexpected time to deal with teenage and young adult drama?

After staring at the paper for a while hoping a solution would jump out at me, I realized that no solution was going to jump out to quantify these. So I did something that I did at work when I had to put together a quantitative business case but had absolutely no data. I made some shit up and hoped it would stick. That would be good enough to start.

When my overanalysis was done, my first pass required a twenty-nine-hour day to complete everything I had prioritized. If nothing else, I had found a way mathematically to violate the laws of physics. No one said work-life balance was going to be easy, but I never thought that my overanalysis would lead me to an impossibility. If you find yourself in the same situation—one where your priorities list results in more hours than there are in a real day—it doesn't mean that you can't add or that you need to start over. As it happened to me, I realized that there was something valuable about coming up with a twenty-nine-hour day. It showed me that I either had to recalculate how much time was needed to achieve these priorities or rethink my priorities. You might also need to do one or the other—or both. (In my case, my twenty-nine-hour day didn't even factor in the many times I would be doing two things at once, like driving to a soccer game while talking to a client).

For me, getting to a day that had a reasonable number of hours and also allowed for at least seven hours of sleep took a number of permutations and more breaks to walk around in circles at the library eating Cheez-Its than I had expected. As you do this, recognize that this is a highly iterative process. Figuring out a future state that is both tangible and doable doesn't usually happen in one shot. For me, it took several empty Cheez-It boxes and some noticeable frustration.

During that process, I had three realizations that can help you reconcile your numbers:

*Realization #1: **Work-life balance isn't just about having the right number of priorities that take the right number of hours. It is about using the hours you have for the right priorities that directly line up with your vision.***

The example I kept coming back to revolved around the significant number of hours I had allocated per day for hard teenage stuff (knowing that some days those hours wouldn't exist and other days those hours would be significant). Those were inevitably going to be emotionally draining hours. Maybe because of that and because I was tired of being so tired, I kept trying to pull those hours out of the equation. Yanking them would reduce the total number of hours in my day. There you go. I would have solved my problem. But my vision wasn't only about making my day shorter. My work-life balance vision was to ensure that I could focus on the right things both at work and in life, even if at select times the total amount of hours for my work-life balance day was still high. I had to put the right number of hours where they belonged, even if it didn't shorten my day each and every day. I'd still have work-life balance. Just not in the way I had thought it was supposed to be before going deep. Which led me to my second realization.

Realization #2: Better work-life balance doesn't always mean having more fun.

This realization was kind of a bummer for me. Going into this exercise, I had a vision of work-life balance that looked like the life of Darryl from AP. Lots of vacations, lots of fun, good times all around. No stress. Beer. Bad karaoke. Beaches disproportionately represented. It was the Carnival cruise of work-life balance. Realistically, that sounded more like retirement than my current stage in life. Breaking through that fictional version of work-life balance is necessary. Of course, all of us could use more time to lounge around, but as you do the work-life math, real balance may equate to time being dedicated to things that are the most important at work and in life but not necessarily those things that feel like a Carnival cruise. For me, it was carving out the time for stressful teenage situations without becoming stressed out because *that* time was taking away from time to grow the business. If I stuck with my priorities, I could do that.

By this point, I knew that focusing on my priorities would come at the expense of growing my business, and that realization hurt. It was a trade-off I had never had to consider—until I broke my priorities down to hours in a day. The math didn't lie. But as long as allocating hours to hard family and life priorities didn't come at the expense of *maintaining* my business, I could make this trade-off, assuming my wife and I were both comfortable with these financial implications. And if I did go forward this way, it was going to be a difficult emotional change. Accepting that my business growth goals would have to be deprioritized or postponed until another stage in life when I could accommodate them stung a little. But keeping the business at status quo, or even slightly reduced for a while, had to be acceptable. I felt fortunate to be able to make this choice at this point in my life. At a different point in my life, I may not have been able to make this kind of choice. Given where you are in your lives, you may or may not have the independence or luxury to make this kind of financial decision, but all of us dads do have the ability to choose the time we do control.

At this point in your work-life visioning, you may also be confronted with work and life trade-offs you've never had to consider before. The math makes those trade-off conversations inevitable. That's what makes this process simultaneously invaluable and frustrating as hell. Ten years ago, when I worked a more traditional job and we had just assumed parental responsibilities for Dani and Gabe, a trade-off choice would have involved taking that next promotion for the increased revenue but at the expense of time at home. It would have been an equally difficult decision to make. And twenty years earlier, when I was just starting out professionally, it would have looked different too. At that point, my career ascension was very important to me. Being in sustaining mode with my career wouldn't have been a trade-off I would have been willing to accept at that time of my life. Now it was.

Realization #3: **_Work-life balance isn't always a fifty-fifty proposition._**

My answers to my more detailed questions skewed more heavily to the life side of the equation. Yours may skew one way or the other too. In my own naivete, I repeatedly tried to "fix" my answers to bring the work and life priorities back into equal balance because that's how I thought they should be. In everything I had read about work-life balance, the concept was depicted graphically as a scale with equal amounts on both sides. Maybe I'm too much of a literalist because that graphic seemed to be predisposing me to the wrong answer. Don't let it predispose you to the wrong answer. My reality right now is that my balance is likely a sixty-five-thirty-five proposition, skewed to the life side. That's what it

needs to be right now, and I have to be okay with that. Yours may be the same or it might be skewed the other way. And at other points in your life, it might be reversed, and that is okay too. What matters is that the skewing feels like the right level of balance you need right now—even if it is eighty-twenty favoring the work side. Whatever popped out as most important in your priorities should be reflected in your work-life vision. A fifty-fifty scale, quite honestly, doesn't seem to be incredibly realistic these days.

Here's what all of this work did for me: I wasn't shooting in the dark anymore, trying to hit a work-life balance target I couldn't even see. I had clarity. It had taken an entire day wandering around the local library to get there. Now it was time to move the vision from theory into reality. As I lead you into my personal journey, I'll issue my first of many CAUTION: MISTAKES AHEAD warnings.

Hamsters Running Around in Old Wheels

If you define your vision but don't change your behaviors to support it, you'll never achieve it.

Once I had finished my detailed work-life vision, I wish that I could report that the next few weeks of my life were the most gloriously balanced weeks I had ever experienced. I wish I could say that I was living on a cloud and everything work and life had to offer suddenly fell into place like a dream. I wish I could say that I found myself whistling a lot more and smiling at total strangers even while they were trying to steal my parking space or cut in line. Unfortunately, the cloud I was living on still had a lot of thunder left in it, and nothing work and life threw at me fell into place at all, which might have explained why the only whistling I did was of angry grunge-rock songs making me want to relive my old mosh pit days at rock concerts. Life wasn't suddenly rainbows and butterflies.

The reality was that my life was no different than before I had taken time to figure out my work-life vision. I was still busy as hell. I was still running around like the proverbial chicken with its head cut off. (Fortunately, the proverbial chicken wasn't one of our eight chickens). I was still stressed and tired. Life kept moving, and it kept moving fast. I had left on a business trip the very next day. When I returned, things just fell back into what they had been. It wasn't as though I had forgotten about my new work-life vision. It was implementing it that was hard.

Even though I had made progress during that day of visioning, I felt further away from the holy grail than ever before. To understand what was going wrong, I again considered methods that I used with my clients. Maybe there was another tie-in here. We often spent time figuring out the company's North Star. What was the company trying to accomplish? We'd work tirelessly to articulate their goals in a compelling way. After long meetings around strategy and direction, clients would leave feeling very optimistic, much like I had after my work-life balance visioning. Months later, many would come back to me frustrated that they weren't making any progress on getting there, much like I was feeling at this point in my personal journey. In fact, they were often demoralized because they now had a vision but, for whatever reason, couldn't seem to turn their vision into reality. I was their consultant and "outside eyes" and could clearly see the problem they were having because I wasn't mired in their day-to-day business operations:

> *If the company's processes, systems, infrastructure, and behaviors weren't aligned with their new vision, they'd never achieve it. Instead, these unaligned processes and behaviors would actually work against the company's new vision.*

I saw this a lot with companies in the business world. Figure out a great vision. Change nothing else about how the company operates. Wonder why we didn't get anywhere.

I had a similar problem with my work-life vision and my initial failure in making it a reality. I had figured out my work-life North Star. Then I had gone out and picked up right where I had left off before figuring that out. If there is one silver lining in this, it's for you to see the mistake I made and not replicate it. Don't think that just because you now have a great work-life vision that it will materialize on its own without substantial changes in everything you are doing every day. I had forgotten that, despite how frequently I have worked with clients on the exact same issue. It was a little embarrassing, but my embarrassment can be your benefit. I'm a giving person.

So how do you move forward so that you don't fall back into the same old hamster wheel? This is where you can go back to your day-in-the-life scenarios to identify the behaviors and trends you saw that need some reconciliation. Earlier, you had put that day-in-the-life aside so you wouldn't work on changing things without knowing what your work-life North Star was. Now that you have your new vision, you can focus on the day-to-day behaviors and habits that might be standing in your way of achieving that specific vision. At this point in my own path towards work-life balance, I did a quick mental inventory of a number of Vortex days, running through them from start to finish, including the day-in-the-life that I was now simply calling "Poopgate." I reviewed my four initial observations (my to-do list was too long, my day had no blank space, I was a human pinball, and I had no plan) and saw trends in the habits I used to manage through my day. For years, those behaviors had helped me get a lot of shit done pretty successfully. But did they support my new work-life vision? Think about your own habits and behaviors; do they support your North Star?

Just like with my clients, if your habits aren't aligned with your vision, you won't be able to turn your vision into operational reality. For me, that meant that I would continue to live the way I had been living, which, by my back-of-the-napkin calculations, gave me at least a fifty percent chance of suffering another Poopgate-type day in the not-too-distant future. After all, I had years to develop the habits that had led me to the life that I had been leading to date—a successful life for all intents and purposes, but one that resulted in a daily Vortex. To live my vision, I had to solve some very real traps and barriers that had been part of the problem the entire time. I needed to operate differently. You might too.

The first step is to identify the traps you see and be explicit about them. With my situation, I asked myself which of my habits and approaches, if left unchanged, might render my new vision unattainable. By all accounts, I had a good life. We weren't destitute. I was successful at work. I had a great wife and a solid marriage (even though no matter how hard I tried, I couldn't get my wife to agree that *Bill & Ted's Excellent Adventure* was the most underrated movie in the history of filmmaking). We had four great kids, despite the daily ups and downs. I had a great relationship with my mom and sister, and I still had friends who were willing to give me the benefit of the doubt even after years of being MIA. I hadn't been doing anything wrong. No doubt, you have your own successes in your life too. It might seem counterintuitive to start picking apart your success in search of problems. But I forced myself to do just that, and it was invaluable. I kept returning to the challenges my clients faced. When you create a totally new vision of what you want and where you are going—even if you were successful before it—the things that got you to that successful point aren't guaranteed to be the same things necessary for achieving the new vision. This is because *how you are defining success has now changed.*

I did some more overanalysis for you (like I said, I'm a giving person), but this time I took my overanalysis beyond my last ten years of being a dad. I talked to other dads. Some were very focused on ascending the corporate ladder to the C-suite. Others ran their own businesses and had various different situations with their spouse, ex-spouses, and kids. Some had young kids. Others had older kids. Some had jobs that they loved but that required them to travel a lot. I was trying to pick out the common themes all of them faced. I also time traveled back twenty years to when I had entered the workforce as a single guy, starting as a data entry clerk for a shipping company and playing in a band. I wondered if I'd find any similarities between that single guy, the dad I'd been for the last ten years, and the dads I talked to. None of this assessment would qualify as a statistically significant study, but it was qualitative data nonetheless. To my surprise, I found eight traps that had been with me the entire time, many of which could be seen in the other dads too. I wrote down the eight traps in the order of the pain they seemed to be causing me:

1. **The trap of forgetting about yourself:** the mistake of unintentionally making yourself the odd man out with all that work and life entailed

2. **The trap of the superhero syndrome:** the detrimental effects of thinking you can do everything

3. **The trap of artificial urgency:** the tendency to label things as urgent even if they really aren't

4. **The trap of undefined boundaries:** the habit of trying to multitask and blend everything together with no clear lines in the sand

5. **The trap of late nights getting it all done:** the pressure of trying to finish things when you are completely drained after exceedingly long days

6. **The trap of no buffer zone:** the practice of not leaving any time for the unexpected and unanticipated

7. **The trap of constant triage:** the failure of allowing no time to

DEFINING YOUR WORK-LIFE BALANCE END GAME

YOU ≈ WORK ≈ "LIFE"

*What trade-offs are you willing to accept to
create balance across all three areas?*

THE 8 TRAPS

1 - The trap of forgetting about yourself

2 - The trap of the superhero syndrome

3 - The trap of artificial urgency

4 - The trap of undefined boundaries

5 - The trap of late nights getting it all done

6 - The trap of no buffer zone

7 - The trap of constant triage

8 - The trap of chasing time

YOUR WORK-LIFE BALANCE HOLY GRAIL

think about what you really want and need in work and life (and how you are going to fulfill those wants and needs) because you are always fighting fires; in other words, the trap of living in a reactive state

8. **The trap of chasing time:** the tendency to focus on what's next instead of being in the moment and appreciating what you are doing right now

As you think about these traps, a few of them may be front and center for you. Others may feel less relevant based on your own current state. Either scenario is okay, but both warrant some action. For me personally, I had been a major perpetrator of every one of these traps for years, including the weeks since my visioning work, which explains why my work-life balance had not improved. Regardless of whether you deserve a red card like me for violating all of them or just a yellow card for a few infractions, not dealing with these traps will get in the way of your newly defined work-life vision.

Now comes the hardest part: *eliminating these traps in a way that doesn't kill the parts of your work and life that are successful but still helps you move toward your new vision.* In the next chapter, I'll show you how I started addressing these traps—for better and for worse. I say for better and for worse because my starting place seemed logical in theory but turned out to be problematic in reality. I am issuing my second CAUTION: MISTAKES AHEAD notice.

Part III: The Eight Traps

The Trap of Forgetting About Yourself

It is surprisingly easy to make yourself the odd man out of your own work-life equation without even realizing it.

I started with the problem of not doing anything for myself anymore. Maybe it was a delirious act of dad desperation to put myself first, but I thought there was a good case for beginning with me. Not doing anything solely for myself anymore was a huge stress inducer. I used to go to the gym. I used to hike and snowboard. I used to watch baseball games. I used to be an electric violinist and studio musician who had accomplished some pretty cool things by turning a traditionally classical instrument into a heavy grunge weapon of musical destruction.

Now I had gained twenty pounds, hadn't set foot on a mountain with or without snow in several years, checked in on baseball games only every once in a while on my cell phone within the sacred walls of the bathroom, and could only reminisce about my previous musical escapades. I wasn't hoping to relive the "good old days." My current life was by far the good days. Yet, those activities had fulfilled me as an individual, and I had allowed them to vanish. I wasn't allowing any time for my own restoration. I was always running on empty. With no gas in the tank, everything became much harder and dragged that much more. Every day, I felt a little more tired than the day before. In small increments, it was hardly noticeable. Over the accumulation of years, it was massive. Ten years ago, I had been walking around as a fully erect and evolved *Homo sapiens*. Now when I looked at myself in the mirror, I saw a Neanderthal—hunched over and with a surprising amount of nose hair. At some point, this lack of restoration had taken a toll not only on me as an individual but on everything I was doing for my business and my family.

The sizeable gap in my work-life equation was me, in particular my personal needs. Living with that gap had become such a habit that it showed up even when I took my first pass at writing my work-life vision. I was nowhere to be found in that first draft. Or maybe I had me in there at some point but dumped me when forced to ration the hours in the day. Like many of us, I was living under the false idea that if something has to give in a busy schedule, it has to be me and my "self" activities, figuring that eliminating those will have the least negative impact on work and life. In hindsight, it was a little scary that I hadn't been the first person on my mind while developing my work-life vision and that my personal needs had been an afterthought.

Back when my dad was going to bed at midnight and waking up at 4:30 in the morning every day, he was still at the gym at 4:45 a.m. before work. As a teenager, I thought my dad had lost his mind. I thought that it was a generally accepted societal rule that any time before 6:00 a.m., before the sun came up, was understood to be sleeping time. My dad used to laugh when I jokingly confronted him about it. Similar to my current understanding of the bathroom as refuge, I now understood his dawn patrol gym routine. He wasn't crazy at all. He was claiming an hour of the day for himself since he knew that the rest of it wasn't for him and him only.

Claiming time for myself wasn't going to be a cakewalk. My schedule was already packed. After all, running a business translated into what felt like a thousand big and little needs every day. Even if I followed my vision and reduced my business growth aspirations to allow me to focus on the life side of the equation, I still had to bring a certain amount of money into the household. And with our family circus, I couldn't remember one day when something didn't need to get done for someone—ninety-nine times out of a hundred that someone not being me, or my wife for that matter. If there were any rare glorious moments when all four kids were under control, I also had my mom and my sister, a gang of crazy chickens squawking around the backyard, a neurotic dog, and a rabbit who indiscriminately ate things. No matter what I did, I wasn't going to escape the fact that I was still the co-ringleader of our circus. Because I often felt like I had no time to ground myself anymore, I felt more like one of the twelve clowns getting out of the packed clown car, bumbling around like the Keystone Cops while my wife—the real ringleader—tried desperately to keep us all from wandering off into the lion cage. If I could somehow find a way to write myself back into my daily script—even if just minimally like my dad had done—I figured that

I could mitigate my stress and maybe even do a better job running my business and being a dad and husband.

That was the case I made to justify starting with the trap of forgetting about myself. It wasn't a bad business case. Then again, not every business case—even a good one—yields the outputs that it projects. If you work in the business world, you've probably learned that lesson the hard way two or thirteen times like I have. Sometimes, though, it isn't the business case itself that is flawed. It's the environment that renders it unsuccessful. Sometimes, it's as simple as timing. Right initiative. Wrong time. My approach to putting myself back into my work-life equation was probably an example of those challenges, but I just didn't realize it at the time. That's why I highlight the rest of my failed attempt over the next few pages—not to deter you from figuring out how to insert yourself back into your work-life equation—but rather so you can see the negative implications of trying to solve work-life balance issues out of sequence, which I'll talk about later in the book.

My Initial Solution: Add one daily restorative activity (even if my calendar was full)

I knew there were only so many hours in the day, and all of those hours were already claimed by business, family, and maybe some sleep—although over the years sleep seemed to have gotten bumped a lot. None of those things could be eliminated. My calendar was booked solid every day. I thought long and hard until I came up with a counterintuitive idea. I would *add* something, just for me, to my daily agenda. Adding something could be risky, even with the good intention of self-care. Would this break the camel's back? Or would adding something just for me—even if it was on top of a fully booked, double-booked, and generally overbooked schedule—feel restorative simply because I could finally get some time to myself? I was going to find out and was desperate and delirious enough to try it.

I started at work. It seemed like the easier path. I wanted something practical and doable that would offer daily "James detox time" at work. Of course, I could go to the gym at lunch or before work like my crazy-but-not-so-crazy dad used to do, but that wasn't a guarantee and had often been a logistical challenge in a busy work schedule when I had tried it in the past. I wasn't giving up on the gym, but for now I wanted something simpler, a way to get out of the work environment to clear my head—a thirty-minute mental detox. It wasn't exactly the power nap, but I had never really understood what a power nap was anyway. Thirty-minute nap and then time to wake up? That wasn't restorative. Even Ben knew that, and he was only two. A thirty-minute break felt achievable and impactful enough to make a difference. Then again, a mini detox didn't make me any money, so I worried that I might never prioritize it. To force myself to prioritize it, I needed a few strategies. I came up with three:

1. **I would "calendar" it as though it was a meeting I absolutely couldn't miss.**

I wasn't above playing mind games with myself. If I scheduled my break as though it was the most important client meeting of the day and put it in my calendar, maybe I would adhere to it.

2. **I would physically remove myself from the work environment.**

I remembered someone who worked for me in the recent past saying:

"James, it is impossible to think around here."

I understood that implicitly. When I worked at home, even though I could shut the door, it didn't remove me mentally or physically from the distractions that occurred on a minute-by-minute basis there. When you are home with a toddler, a closed door doesn't mean much, other than an opportunity to practice turning the handle to open it or knock incessantly because the noise is really cool. When I was on site with my clients, there wasn't a door to shut most of the time. Regardless of the location, people would come by to talk, the phone would ring, or I would see an e-mail come through and convince myself:

"I'll just respond to this one e-mail, and then I'll tune it out . . ."

Twenty minutes later, I would have done a nice job of responding to all of my e-mails . . . and a few phone calls . . . and helping another leader who stopped by not wanting to interrupt (but did anyway). Being in the environment—whether at home or at work—didn't give me any time to think nor did I get any alone time to restore my brain. Physically leaving the premises was critical for me, even if only to walk around the block.

3. I would leave my cell phone behind.

This would be a daring move for me considering how compulsively I checked it. If I brought my phone with me, with almost one hundred percent certainty, I would receive a text, an e-mail, or a call that would distract me from good thinking time or interrupt solitude time. If by some miracle nothing came in, simply by having my cell phone with me, I'd be tempted to read a new blog post or article about legitimately important news or even something as absurd as the latest New England Patriots conspiracy theories on ESPN about how they've rigged the system to win the next thirteen Super Bowls. As hard as it was going to be to disconnect, this was about giving myself thirty minutes to think, or maybe to not think at all, because as things stood, I never took time for either.

That all seemed doable and sustainable. It was a good plan. Then I moved beyond work hours. I decided to add piano lessons at home. As an ex-musician, I thought I had happily moved on to running my own business and having a big family. What I realized, though, was that in the years since I started the business and the family grew, my love for music was still there but totally ignored. There simply hadn't been enough time. I was now going to make the piano my restorative activity and make time for it by using brute force. No questions asked. This was going to happen. Even though it was only thirty minutes a week for a lesson and a measly thirty minutes a day for practice, it still felt daunting. Nevertheless, I would give it a shot. I was going to learn how to play the piano. And I was going to enjoy it, dammit. And it was going to be restorative, dammit. Even if it killed me.

Putting it all into action

I was cautiously optimistic that "James detox time" would help me at work, and my optimism wasn't unfounded. I regularly took my thirty-minute daily zone-out time. I left the environment. I left my cell phone behind. Sometimes, I walked around the block. Sometimes, I sat in the car and listened to music. At first, I felt like I did when I used to ditch school, a little guilty. Still, a mere thirty minutes made a huge difference at work. It was like I was starting the day over. It was that restorative. Had I known about this years ago, I would have been doing it for decades.

I was even more excited about playing the piano, wondering how restorative that might be. I practiced piano every night at 9:00, after work was done, Jen and the kids had gone to bed, the rabbit was secured in the garage, the chickens were back in the coop, and the dog was worn out from barking. At that hour, I wasn't exactly overflowing with energy, then an awesome thing happened. Despite adding piano to my already packed schedule, I actually felt restored when I went to bed, and when I woke up the next morning. I loved my alone time to play. It was relaxing. I wasn't thinking about anything other than playing. Given that initial success, you might be wondering why I issued a bold CAUTION: MISTAKES AHEAD notice a few pages ago. Let's just say that things didn't end well.

For a few weeks, I did experience a feeling of relief and restoration. Unfortunately, life continued to happen. Babies got sick, toddlers had toddler issues, teenagers had teenager issues (which sometimes seemed strikingly similar to toddler issues), business needs arose unexpectedly. Barely into the piano experiment, my 9:00 p.m. piano time turned into 11:00 p.m. piano time and having to play really quietly because it was so late. Sometimes, it turned into imagining myself playing the piano and tapping my fingers on the sink while sitting in the bathroom. I realized that I couldn't play piano every day as I had hoped. And the days when I couldn't play felt harder than before I had taken up the piano—now I knew what I was missing. If I needed any indication that there were too many obstacles working against my "me time," this was it. I have a small personality flaw, though. I'm a little stubborn. I didn't want to let piano playing or my restorative activity die. Instead of abandoning ship, I concluded that playing piano couldn't be my *only* restorative activity.

I looked for other activities to supplement the piano when I couldn't play—kind of like creating a cafeteria plan of restorative activities. It certainly made sense, as long as my cafeteria plan included smaller "bite-sized" activities. I came up with things as simple as reading one *Far Side* cartoon every morning. I had always been a demented Gary Larson fan. I even found a compilation of every *Far Side* cartoon Gary Larson had ever written. I could read one cartoon every morning as my new bite-sized morning ritual that would carry me through the day. Maybe I could even read another one before bed. I also added some gym time to the cafeteria plan so that I wouldn't turn around in two years to find that I had put on another twenty pounds. The cafeteria plan was in place: piano, gym, *The Far Side*. One may not have been viable on any given day, but I assumed that another one would be. To make a long story short, it was a better concept, but it didn't work either. I was officially zero for two.

The problem came down to sustainability. On the work side, my thirty-minute daily zone-out time felt very sustainable. I was continuing to do it, with good results and impact. Unfortunately, the same couldn't be said for the piano playing, gym time, or even the easy thirty-second *Far Side* reads. They all fell by the wayside within a month. At that point, Gabe ended up playing the piano more than I did (and he didn't play that much), the *Far Side* book stared at me—unopened—every morning, and I was barely doing two days at the gym—my workouts were a short-and-sweet thirty minutes when I got lucky. Why did my restorative activities at home fall apart again? And why weren't they sustainable?

It wasn't that my solution wasn't broad or flexible enough. I still think that my cafeteria plan idea was pretty creative. The problem was that in every confrontation between the restorative activity and a packed schedule, the packed schedule won. It was like Mickey Mouse taking on Muhammad Ali. It wasn't a fair fight. In no way was I giving up on the notion of implementing a sustainable restorative activity for myself. You shouldn't let my implementation mistake deter you from doing that, either, because incorporating something that you really love to do into your day is invaluable. For me, it was a requirement if I was ever going to find my work-life holy grail, but the lesson here is that adding your own personal needs into the work-life balance equation can't happen in a vacuum. In other words, the trap of forgetting about yourself can't be fixed as a stand-alone without first fixing the packed schedule problem and any other obstacles that get in the way of time for a restorative activity. For that matter, none of the eight traps can be viewed by themselves. I tell you the story about my failure with my restorative activities to point out that trying to pick off the traps one at a time has a high likelihood of failure. Because of that, let's now look at the eight traps a little differently than from a sequential standpoint. But don't lose hope for restorative activities. By the end of the book, there will be plenty of space for it.

Looking at the Eight Traps Differently

The eight traps are actually a system and must be addressed collectively, not individually.

Initially, I tried solving the eight traps by simply selecting the biggest pain point for me. That approach certainly seems logical. Solve the thing that feels the worst first. That's not an entirely bad approach; businesses use that approach all the time, but only with limited success, unfortunately. The reason: the traps have causal links to each other— some traps cause other traps. In other words, some are symptoms, and some are root causes. If you try to eliminate the symptoms first, you will make only surface-level improvements, if any at all. That's why jumping to pain points gets only limited success. You have to find the root causes of the pain points. It is no different than if a physician treated only symptoms instead of the underlying health challenges that are causing those symptoms. Therefore, finding the root cause traps should make the other traps disappear or at least mitigate them significantly. To understand how these traps work as a system, I'll show you how this relates to some of the work I do with my clients.

First, I'll come clean and admit that sometimes people in my field of business consulting get a bad rap for two things. One is coming up with really weird terms for saying normal everyday things. The other is for taking what seem like simple things and making them more complicated than they need to be. I certainly didn't want to do that in my search for work-life balance—or yours—but there is some inherent complexity in this. With a good number of my clients, we often talk about "systems thinking"—or the ability to see how all of the pieces fit together holistically, how inputs to one area impact outputs to other areas. Without it, you solve problems in one area that might not help the bigger picture. Worse, you might even create unforeseen problems in other areas. It happens all the time, which is probably why I have a consulting practice that is still in business eight years after I started it. The good news is that I'm pretty good at helping companies with these problems. The bad news is that I had failed to apply that same systems thinking to my work-life balance problem. My bad news is your good news. You don't need to follow me down that path.

Instead, you can view the eight traps as a system from the get-go. For me, understanding how one trap impacts another was now critical if I was going to reach the Darryl from AP work-life balance Hall of Fame status. As it stood after my initial failure, I was pretty sure I was about to be sent back down to the minor leagues. Before I tweak the methodology, let's review the eight traps—in order of how I had identified them, which was based on the pain point principle of identifying the one that hurt the most:

1. **The trap of forgetting about yourself:** the mistake of unintentionally making yourself the odd man out with all that work and life entailed

2. **The trap of the superhero syndrome:** the detrimental effects of thinking you can do everything

3. **The trap of artificial urgency:** the tendency to label things as urgent even if they really aren't

4. **The trap of undefined boundaries:** the habit of trying to multitask and blend everything together with no clear lines in the sand

5. **The trap of late nights getting it all done:** the pressure of trying to finish things when you are completely drained after exceedingly long days

6. **The trap of no buffer zone:** the practice of not leaving any time for the unexpected and unanticipated

7. **The trap of constant triage:** the failure of allowing no time to think about what you really want and need in work and life (and how you are going to fulfill those wants and needs) because you are always fighting fires; in other words, the trap of living in a reactive state

8. **The trap of chasing time:** the tendency to focus on what's next instead of being in the moment and appreciating what you are doing right now

My new perspective on systems thinking brought clarity; overanalysis was unnecessary. I scribbled out a model on the back of an envelope I was supposed to be using to pay a bill for my company. Then my business consultant side took over and turned it into a PowerPoint flowchart (p. 72).

Even though this flowchart is more complex than my original depiction of the eight traps problem, this view makes the problem legitimately solvable because it shows that you have to start in the right place and sometimes even solve for several barriers at once. Looking at the new version of the methodology, by starting with the trap of forgetting about myself, I had inadvertently started at the end of the equation. As I looked at my systems flowchart and reflected on my Vortex days (Poopgate included), I saw very clearly what was happening:

> I thought I could do everything (**superhero syndrome**) and was constantly throwing in new urgent things because of my tendency to classify everything as urgent (**artificial urgency**), resulting in a list of eighteen things to do every day. Combined with the fact that I wasn't setting any formal boundaries (**undefined boundaries**) and was trying to multitask and blend it all together in some sort of circus juggling act, I ended up rushing from place to place because of a completely overbooked calendar (**no buffer zone**), which put me in reactive mode (**constant triage**), which then had me just trying to get shit done, checking the next box and always thinking about what else had to get done (**chasing time**). Since there were so many items on my to-do list, my days got longer and longer (**late nights getting it all done**) until there was no room to do anything for myself (**forgetting about yourself**). This was why I lived in the Vortex, perpetually exhausted by my blurry life.

As you run through your own traps in this more linear flow, you might find similar challenges for the same reasons. Or you might find a similar flow but with different nuances that are specific to your work-life challenges. You might also find that only certain parts of the flowchart seem at first glance to be relevant to you.

So now back to the question of how to get started with the traps. To really get at this, you need to start with the three areas that have the

THE 8 TRAPS –
"A SYSTEM CREATING IMBALANCE"

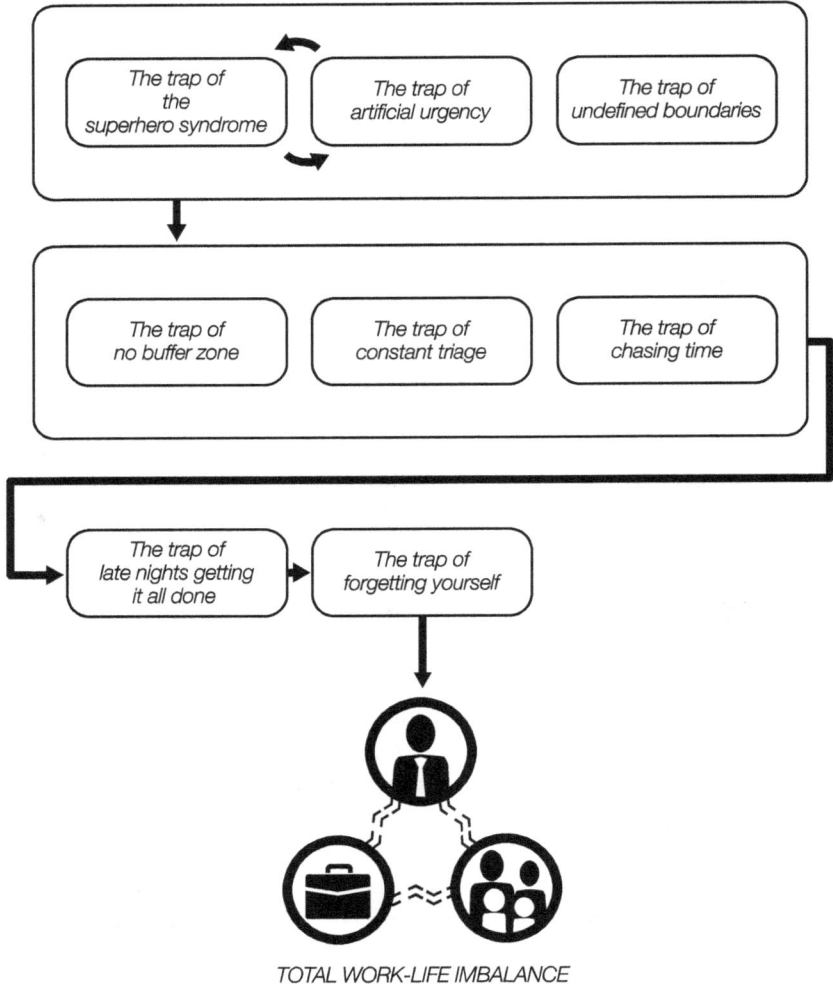

The trap of
the
superhero syndrome

The trap of
artificial urgency

The trap of
undefined boundaries

The trap of
no buffer zone

The trap of
constant triage

The trap of
chasing time

The trap of
late nights getting
it all done

The trap of
forgetting yourself

TOTAL WORK-LIFE IMBALANCE

highest likelihood of driving mass work-life hysteria into the rest of the equation (the trap of the superhero syndrome, the trap of artificial urgency, and the trap of undefined boundaries)—even if those aren't areas that seem like major problems for you right now. One of the things I've learned the hard way from this kind of systems thinking in my work is that it is easy to underestimate or not even realize some causal elements until you dive into them. That's again part of the reason for the day-in-the-life assessment. Those first three traps may be contributing to some downstream traps in ways you haven't realized. My business clients experience that all the time.

For the remainder of the book, I'm going to work through the traps in the order of the systems flow chart, which was exactly how I worked them in my year-long journey and after my initial restorative activity failure. For me, the first two traps (the superhero syndrome and artificial urgency) worked together to wreak havoc. In parallel, I also needed to solve the trap of undefined boundaries because if my Poopgate day-in-the-life had shown me anything, it was that being a human pinball caused way too much stress. If I nailed these three traps, I had a feeling that the other traps might recede as a result of addressing the root causes. It was time to try to talk some sense into a well-intentioned but overly urgent superhero dad. You might know the type.

Wreaking Havoc on Work-Life Balance: The Traps of the Superhero Syndrome and Artificial Urgency

By trying to urgently do everything, you forego the two most important requirements for work-life balance— prioritization and acceptance of trade-offs.

Before going any further, I'll give you a brief flashback to my life before fatherhood. My intention is to illustrate my historical approach to work and life for as long as I've been part of the workforce. The behaviors are what matter in this flashback. You'll be able to see what I needed to change.

Early in my career, my goal was to ascend the corporate ladder. I was never told by my mom or dad that I had to become vice president in a big company at a relatively young age, but that was what I had assumed career success meant, and so I put myself on that path. I turned out to be pretty good in the business world. At the same time, I was also a young, aspiring musician with two bands and side gigs of studio recording work. At that point, work-life balance consisted of churning hard by day in my corporate job and then playing shows, doing studio recordings, and pursuing anything and everything else I could in my music world. The rest of my time was focused on friends. Friends were the other life part of the work-life equation for me at the time. Sleep sometimes happened, but it seemed incidental because I wasn't about to compromise anything. I was young and found a way to do it all.

On one occasion, younger me flew to Dallas from Los Angeles early one morning for an all-day business meeting, caught a late-afternoon flight back to Los Angeles to play a late-night show at the then notorious Viper Room in Hollywood, only to haul back to the Los Angeles airport to make a red-eye return flight to Dallas so I could be back by mid-morning for our follow-up half-day business meeting. I worked all night on the plane to finalize my part of a presentation due the next day. When the meeting was over and my presentation was complete, I rerouted my flight back home through Chicago so that I could visit a friend of mine from school who I hadn't seen in a while. When I arrived there, I crashed on her couch for an hour before going out and hitting the Chicago social scene until 4:00 a.m. In hindsight, that three-day schedule might sound absurd, but that was my standard operating procedure back then. I was going to do it all. I was "all in" on all fronts. As I saw it, nothing could be deprioritized. All was going to get done. That Dallas client sent complimentary e-mails to my boss in the consulting firm, saying things like:

"Sudakow is an absolute machine" or "This guy can carry more work on his shoulders than anyone I've ever seen."

The client didn't even know about my late-night musical escapades on top of the work I was doing for his company. Of course, he was getting e-mails from me at two in the morning, so of course he thought I was a machine. On my end, I would often jump back into work mode late at night after getting home from a show. It was as though I led a double life—buttoned-up corporate guy by day, alternative grunge rock violinist by night. Sometimes, I'd have my laptop with me at shows. While my bandmates drank beer, talked to girls, and generally put out the cool band vibe, I'd be finishing PowerPoint presentations and sending work e-mails from a dark booth that smelled just funny enough to motivate me to finish my work.

That was then. The flashback is over. Now I'm older but am still a machine who operates the same way. If I had any doubts about that, all I had to do was revisit one of my typical Vortex days. When everything work and life threw at me piled up, my solution was simply to haul it on my shoulders like a machine and do it all:

- Big client strategic planning meeting today? Get it done.

- Take Ben to swimming lessons? Get it done.

- Go to and pick up Gabe from his club volleyball game? Get it done.

- Work out at the gym? Get it done? Maybe. Okay, get it done. Can't let it slide.

- Respond to all work e-mails? Get it done.

- Put that big presentation together for my client meeting on Monday? Get it done.

- Have that call with a potential new client? Get it done.

- Draft a statement of work based on that call for prospective new business? Get it done.

- Play with Ivan? Get it done. Did I really just say "get it done" to playing with my three-month-old son?

- Eat a good meal? Get it . . . well . . . eat a jar of almonds so I can claim victory on protein intake for the day while ensuring I don't get a headache from lack of nourishment? Get it done.

- Go to bed completely wasted? Definitely got that done.

- Wake up tomorrow refreshed and ready to roll again? Not done.

If this all feels eerily familiar to you, I'm glad to have the company. (If you don't see yourself in the flashback or the Vortex, you may have already found the holy grail of work-life balance, which means I'm coming over to your house for an exclusive dinner interview.) If you are like me, you are probably getting it all done just like I have been able to do. Because of that, if an agent from the soon-to-be-created Federal Bureau of Work-Life Balance showed up to audit our work and lives, everything would probably seem in order, even successful. For me, business stuff was all getting done. Family stuff was all getting done. I was the partner to my wife I wanted to be in the house and raising the kids. Baby Ivan was doing great. Ben was doing awesome too. The two older kids were figuring out life as teenagers often do: in a way that frustrates their parents (the role we were playing). But they were figuring it out nonetheless, despite bouts of typical teenage drama, including predictable defiance around parental authority, dabbling in strange things and substances with their friends, inexperienced-driver car accidents, and general emotional ups and downs, as well as the seemingly repetitive conversation where we say numerous times a week: "As long as you live here, you aren't going to do *that!*" So as the expression goes, "All's well that ends well," right?

Unfortunately, it is not ending well. Otherwise, you wouldn't be reading this book, and I wouldn't have written it. Grinding through work and life leaves collateral damage. That collateral damage is often you—physical exhaustion coupled with emotional exhaustion. Every day, you check all of the big and little boxes. Doing that not only leaves you depleted and unable to fill the tank back up to even a quarter full, but it also has a more significant effect: with so many things to do every day, finding enjoyment in any of them becomes nearly impossible. Put your head down. Crank it out. In some ways, the ability to find a way to do everything—a trait that has given many of us great success to this point in our work and home lives and one that is *rewarded* in the work world (making it all that much harder to change)—may be the very thing that could bring us down in the end. There is a lot of research out there these days about the long-term health damage caused by subjecting yourself to the levels of stress required to regularly do everything. I think back on Poopgate. The entire day was one big adrenaline rush just to get through it. I was in fight-or-flight mode all day. And then I did it the next day. And the day after that.

Maybe long lists of things to do and the stress related to crazy schedules is inherent to being a working dad these days. Everything needs to be done. That's our jobs as dads, isn't it? Do the work. Then coach the peewee basketball team. Then do the work. Then help with homework. That's what my dad probably would have said if I had been able to get up at 4:30 in the morning to do some dad-son bonding at the gym and ask him about it between bench press sets. But if you get it all done but are a complete basket case, have you really succeeded at work-life balance?

The trap of artificial urgency "eggs you on" and feeds into your superhero syndrome

Then there is a compounding effect. Other than blaming personal hardwiring and DNA, why do many of us feel this need to do everything?

I'm not even the classic Type-A personality. If you are one of those types, I won't hold it against you. My dad was, and he and I were close all the way until he passed. The bottom line is that most of us set high standards for ourselves in our work and desire to be the best husbands and dads we can be. Most of us want to get good things done, and most of us don't want it to take forever to do them. There's nothing wrong with that. Again, it has made most of us successful. There is a natural urgency about how we live and work these days. Even more so at work where acting with urgency seems to be an unstated rule. I can't remember the last time I heard a client say that we should move slowly. The important question to ask here is this:

> *Is acting with urgency at work becoming such a habit that you now bring that sense of urgency home and let it drive how you live the other parts of your life?*

As I thought more about the superhero syndrome and the detrimental effects of trying to do everything, I wondered not just about what any of us achieve but the journey required to achieve it. And that led me back to the inevitable question of stress. When I looked back at some of my best achievements in my career—including building a successful business—they all came with a lot of stress. Were those achievements worth the stress? With building my business, there wasn't a simple answer when it came down to the costs and benefits. I recalled my third, fourth, and fifth years in business. On paper, those were glory years. I grew the business substantially and fast. I had revenue beyond what I had ever imagined—to the point where it didn't even feel real. Even with this awesome business achievement, I also vividly remembered telling my wife that I was never, ever, ever going to do those three years again. I had too many clients with too many demands. To establish my consulting practice, I had swung at every pitch that had come my way and had even run out and thrown myself a few softballs so that I could hit them too. I had subcontractors working all over the place for me, and all I was doing was trying to keep the bullet train from careening off the tracks, which it seemed to be perilously close to doing almost every day. Business was booming, and I could easily cite those years as the most successful years of my business, except when it came to my mental health. For those of you who don't run your own business, my example is no different than taking a big promotion at work and doing the hard work in a new, bigger, and much more challenging but impactful role for your career. You feel good about the value you are providing at work and the trajectory of your career. I had certainly felt that way at every promotion I received on my way up to vice president. The question is at what cost from a stress perspective. And how does this stress relate to how balanced or imbalanced you feel every day?

With my own business example, at the point when I was in the boom years, we didn't have Ivan and Ben yet, but Gabe was twelve, and Dani was sixteen. Even then I was trying to be a work-life superhero. Was it worth it in the end? To this day, I'm not sure. It was highly stressful, and I felt that stress every day. I also felt it every night when I didn't sleep well. It is easy to feel ambivalent about those boom years, though, because I made some great business and financial accomplishments that benefited the family. My role as provider was being fulfilled very well, even though it rendered me a walking zombie for the rest of my dad role, which included soccer tournaments all over the state, youth basketball coaching, volunteer judging of high school speech and debate tournaments, teaching Dani how to drive, and staying on top of Gabe's grades during that very weird development period called middle school. I did all of those things but only through sheer will and in a depleted state.

What those years helped me understand, though, was just how much stress is built into the things we all do and how much of it is unnecessarily manufactured by . . . *ourselves*. In launching my business, for example, how much stress did I create myself because of my aspirations, goals, approach, or even my ego? When it comes to urgency and stress:

> *How much urgency are you creating that isn't inherently there? And how much stress are you then creating by creating your own urgency that isn't inherently there?*

As I was going down my own path toward work-life balance, I remember talking with a friend I hadn't see in a while who had stopped by unexpectedly. She worked for a small global fashion company, traveled a lot, and had a son who was Gabe's age. She had stopped by the house on a day when Jen and I were both home, just to see how the kids were doing. She was a good family friend. Our conversation started with the same caveats that most of my conversations with friends seem to start these days:

"I'm sorry that I haven't stopped by lately. Things have been crazy. So much going on."

"No problem. It's been the exact same thing for us lately."

For me, "lately" was just a euphemism for "all the time" since using the word "lately" gave me false hope that this was just a temporary phenomenon. Our friend told us about all she had to do by the end of the week. I then told her all I had piled up for my company and family in the next few days. Then I somewhat flippantly said:

"Hey, aren't these deadlines artificial anyway? Didn't we just create them for ourselves?"

There was a moment of unexpected silence. There might have been some truth in that thought. As an experiment, we both looked at our lists of things that absolutely, unquestionably, unequivocally needed to be done within the urgent time frames we had set or something horrific would happen. Maybe that horrific thing wasn't going to be the end of the world as we knew it, but it would inevitably be something close to that because there was no reason to be acting with such urgency if the consequences weren't dire.

As I scanned my eighteen-item list, my initial reaction was that they were all urgent. If they weren't urgent, they wouldn't be on the list, of course. Then I looked at them again. If I was going to be honest with myself, only about 25 percent of my tasks warranted real urgency. I had been stressing out about the majority of my list when the reality was that my business and family life were in no way going to be adversely affected if those things got done tomorrow or even next week. *I had manufactured due dates, and as a result, I had manufactured my own stress.* This resulted in an overly long to-do list, which, coupled with the

superhero syndrome of getting it all done caused me to feel like I didn't have work-life balance.

> **The traps of the superhero syndrome and artificial urgency fundamentally fuel each other. Too much urgency creates too many things to do. Too many things to do coupled with a mindset that you will get all of those too many things done at all costs results in the feeling that you are drowning and have no balance.**

Let's be realistic about this, though. In the workplace, you probably experience artificial urgency almost everywhere. Unfortunately, artificial urgency in that environment probably isn't going away any time soon. Large initiatives have deadlines. Sometimes, there are financial and strategic implications for those deadlines. Sometimes there really aren't. We all just want to move with urgency. Sometimes, we do that because of the pressures we feel about our own careers. Sometimes, we do that because of the pressures we feel from others who are feeling the pressures of their own careers. With that pressure comes stress. And that stress doesn't stop with us individually. It gets distributed to everyone else who is involved in the work, which then creates a cascade of stress over other work projects or activities that are peripherally impacted. I was certainly guilty of that in my business. You could at least justify it in the workplace, even if it wasn't right. But I was equally guilty of urgency in my personal life, giving myself deadlines for things that didn't need them. I had gotten so used to urgent deadlines that I applied them by habit and without thought. There's enough real urgency and real stress at work and in life without adding unnecessary stress by creating unnecessary urgency.

So how do you solve this problem? In some ways, you have to solve both traps at the same time since they work together to cause work-life balance problems. Solving the trap of the superhero syndrome without solving the trap of artificial urgency won't really get you anywhere. In the spirit of what may really drive what, let's start with addressing artificial urgency. That's where I started.

Solution—Part 1: Urgency filters

It may seem basic, but without some way of determining what constitutes legitimate urgency, you run the risk of making too many things urgent simply by default—at work and at home. I realized that it came down to urgency filters, a simple set of questions to help you test your perception of urgency with valid criteria. Here are the first two questions to ask:

1. **Why do you think this task or activity you are doing is urgent?**

2. **Why are you choosing this deadline for this task or activity?**

When I applied these two questions to my to-do list, I found that I didn't know why I had chosen some of the deadline dates other than because I either wanted the task done so I didn't have to think about it anymore or because I had created some scenario where I had convinced myself that bad things would happen if it didn't get done. That was the best reasoning I could come up with.

Asking yourself the "why" questions are as good a place to start as anywhere. You then need to go deeper. While the "why" questions can prompt you to think about the activity before ascribing urgency automatically, you also need criteria that is relevant to you to decide what constitutes urgency. As I was developing my own urgency filters, I realized that the specific criteria might be very different in determining true urgency for work and for life. As I often did in my work-life balance journey, I started with work. It always felt like more familiar turf for applying a methodology like this. As much as I tried to overanalyze my work urgency criteria, it turned out that I needed only one question:

Will there be any significant degradation to my business— in particular, financially—if I don't respond to this request right now or do this task or activity right now?

Or for those of you who work for someone else:

Will there be any significant degradation to the work you are responsible for—from a budget, time, quality, or relational perspective—if you don't respond to this request right now or do this task or activity right now?

Ultimately, whether you run your own business or work for someone else, the key is to figure out the question or questions that help you put the right criteria front and center for making an objective decision about urgency.

For me, it came down to financial impact. Since I am my family's sole financial provider, my business needed to bring in a certain amount of money. My decisions around what was urgent and what wasn't couldn't negatively impact that threshold. All of this work towards trying to change behaviors to support my new work-life vision wouldn't be worth anything if the outcome was an inability to bring in a certain baseline amount of money to support our family needs. I had defined that threshold in my vision but needed to carefully examine every decision around urgency so I could understand how it impacted that threshold. Even if you don't run your own business, your work is your livelihood too. Your decisions around what is urgent and what isn't urgent can't negatively impact your livelihood and family needs.

Figuring out an urgency filter on the life side is admittedly more challenging. There was of course the matter of life, death, and sickness, but those felt too obvious. I personally thought I needed filters beyond the obvious because it seemed all too easy to act with urgency for all family matters—often at the expense of my work—simply because I cared so much about my family. The list was endless on the types of things I habitually labeled as urgent. The volleyball game was urgent. Booking next year's family vacation by the end of the week was urgent. Yes, I really just said that. Now that I was taking a harder look at how I managed my life, I found it just a little weird that I had been such a hard-driving family vacation booker. Wasn't planning a vacation supposed to be a fun experience? Not for me. We were booking by "X date" if it killed me. And if it did kill me, I had a plan for who would get my ticket, of course. The point is to take a look your personal life to see what unnecessary urgency habits you may have brought home from work. Spillover happens more easily than you might think.

What if it was as simple as saying that the only real urgency on the life front was health? I considered how that would play out for me compared to what I used to claim was urgent.

- **Booking the family vacation?** Used to be really, really, really urgent. Wouldn't be urgent anymore. Come back to reality.

- **Getting to every soccer game?** Used to be urgent. Wouldn't be urgent anymore. Still worth a big effort, though.

- **Dropping work to get to Ivan's regular doctor's appointment?** Used to be urgent. Maybe it wasn't actually urgent. Maybe it wasn't critical that both my wife and I go. My urgency came because I wanted to be a good dad and part of Ivan's life so badly that I may have been mislabeling the appointment as urgent. But with more and more of us doing preschool drop-offs and fulfilling other family needs during the workweek, maybe we can give ourselves the benefit of the doubt that we are good dads—even if we don't make it to every doctor's appointment.

- **Responding to teenage drama and mental health?** Used to be urgent. Probably still about as urgent as it gets. Proactively helping a teenager navigate the challenging world of adolescence was still the highest of priorities and was often going to mean urgent responses.

I looked at only four things. You have your own specifics about what you are deeming urgent in your personal life that ultimately you have to reconcile. The only way to really find out is to start thinking about each one and asking the questions. For me, three of my four couldn't be classified as code red anymore based on the health filter. The takeaway from this life urgency filter exercise as I see it is:

Confusing "want" and "need" is even easier at home that it is at work. These are our families. We may want to do everything for them, but we may not need to. Ascribing "need" too frequently leads to unnecessary urgency.

Additionally, life urgency and work urgency don't look the same or have the same implications. A lack of urgency at home doesn't mean that you don't care. But at work, it is sometimes seen that way. An employee who lacks urgency may be viewed as unmotivated in the job, not committed to the company, undeserving of a promotion. Employees may feel pressured into urgency just to be viewed in a positive light. I have been in many succession planning leadership meetings where I hear comments such as: "John doesn't really demonstrate any urgency. I wonder how much he really is invested in what he is doing. I am not sure he is leadership material." Maybe at work, those connections are legitimate, although most leaders I speak with really clarify this by wanting employees to focus with urgency on the things that require urgency. This all leads back to work urgency filters.

At home, though, removing urgency doesn't mean that you are not invested in your personal and family responsibilities. It just means that most of those things don't require your immediate action and instead, you can focus on whatever most benefits your family at that moment. In my incorrect thinking, I had been creating urgency as a means of showing I cared when I didn't need to. Everyone knew I cared. It wasn't like work where you feel the pressure—however manufactured that may be—to show your bosses, coworkers, or clients that you care through urgency.

Solution—Part 2: Do only mission critical tasks

Ultimately, work-life balance requires the ability to prioritize, to truly check-out when you say you will, to not respond to everything, to not be there for everyone all of the time, and to accept the implications of certain decisions you may make. Many of us who suffer from the superhero syndrome have a hard time accepting trade-offs and instead convince ourselves that we can do it all. And then we go out and do get it all done, usually with lots of pats on the back but huge amounts of physical and emotional stress.

Similar to urgency, you may need to change your mindset around the value and impact of doing everything. Instead of finding a way to do everything, you may need to find a way to not do everything at work, at home, or even in both places depending on your work-life vision. Doing less may make you feel less accomplished in certain areas of your life, at least initially, compared to what you were doing before. Doing less also offers a high probability of feeling like you aren't maximizing your contribution at work or at home, which may contradict your work ethic and family values. These might be the trade-offs you had never been willing to talk about before.

I'll raise my hand first. All of the above applied to me. Given my new work-life vision, I needed a way to say no to new client opportunities that would feel great for my business ego in terms of exceeding last year's revenue but would put that much more stress on me given everything I needed to be doing at home. My vision had committed to sustainability instead of growth. On the home front, I needed to not say yes to every dynamically changing need. I wasn't good at pulling back in that way. If things needed to change at home and I needed to shift on a dime, I did it. Or I tried. My wife and I still debate just how good I am at shifting on a dime. I think I'm pretty good. She's less impressed.

Because of my desire to be an active part of my family—a key part of my work-life vision—I felt that there were few home needs that I could say no to. As a result, I felt compelled to shift and juggle my schedule to accommodate those sometimes unanticipated family needs. Unfortunately, shifting and juggling could have a negative impact on work, though, which still needed to be done (and done well) because nothing at work was ever eliminated or deprioritized. A work process that had been organized and methodical often became haphazard to accommodate everything on the life front that I was bending over backwards to do. That caused *me* to suffer even if everything for work still got done, often by squeezing work tasks in late at night or before the sun came up the next morning. So the next work-life balance question to ask is:

How do you know what constitutes mission critical?

Urgency filters are a key piece in figuring that out, but you also need a framework for limiting the number of things that could fall into the must-do category. That's where the simple and admittedly arbitrary "rule of three" comes into play. As you have probably figured out by now, one of the key elements in my work-life balance approach is to ask myself hard questions that I had never been willing to ask before and then doing something even harder: accept the implications of my answers. This case was no different. The next question on the list became:

If you could do only three work things and three life things today, what are they?

It was an arbitrary number, but it was a good starting point. Of course, those three things have to line up with your new work-life vision and the corresponding urgency filters you have implemented for yourself. Surprisingly for me, deciding on the three most important work and life things wasn't the hard part. I kind of already knew in my gut what they were, and my urgency filters simply confirmed and validated them. The hard part was accepting not doing the other twelve things on an eighteen-item list. Even though those twelve things weren't the most important and urgent, they were still important. I faced trade-offs I'd never had to make before, and if you force yourself to ask and answer this question honestly, you will too.

Some of mine were significant, like revenue trade-offs for my business. Could I really accept not taking another client when one was right there for the taking? I had never turned away a client in the eight years I had been in business. Would my dad (my greatest mentor) roll over in his grave knowing that I was doing this? How would that impact my business in the long term? The same can be said for you at work. Can you really accept not taking a promotion when it is being handed to you? How many of us would do that? I had never done that in my entire career because I had never been willing to entertain why that would be of any value to anyone (especially me and my view of what my career needed to look like without factoring in the bigger work-life balance picture).

On the family side, could I really accept missing Gabe's volleyball tournament? I had killed myself to be at almost every soccer and volleyball game throughout the years because I wanted to show support. Would he think I didn't care anymore? The same could be said for you if taking that promotion is indeed what you wanted. What life implications of that decision are you willing to accept? Traveling more and being home less are often the obvious ones. Limiting to only three things was hard for me and might be hard for you. Ironically, despite its toll, being a superhero and doing everything was actually easier than this.

The point of the rule of three is forced prioritization. The most successful businesses that I consult with are the ones best at forced prioritization. Some even call it "ruthless prioritization." And applying that same ruthless prioritization to work-life balance might be exactly what you need. Ruthless prioritization helped me stop running around like a maniac and, instead, start enjoying and appreciating both work and life. If I limited myself to the mission critical tasks, maybe I could even enjoy the driving time with Gabe as he logged his hours towards getting his driver's license (as much as anyone can actually enjoy driving around with someone who hasn't yet figured out the proper speed to take turns). I could be present without thinking about the next item on my list or the fact that I still had thirteen things left to do on my list for the day and it was already 6:00 p.m. Maybe I could focus on and find fulfillment in the client meeting I was leading, without feeling rushed or having my attention divided because I had committed to something at home that would survive just fine without me.

Results and Outcomes: How did this all play out?

I started by testing my urgency filters to see if they worked in real life. I had two assumptions for my work urgency filters. The first assumption was that most of the time there wouldn't be a direct and immediate negative financial consequence to reduced urgency in some areas of work. I hoped this would be the case. My other assumption was that I had the inclination to concoct a reason that something was urgent anyway. I hoped this wouldn't be the case. But urgency is a habit. That being said, sometimes at work, urgency is just passed along to you as an unwanted gift, and you have no control over it. I had lived that scenario many times in my career. Someone else's urgency fell into my lap and now became my urgency, and there was very little I could do to change it. Clients do it to me now. Bosses and other business leaders did it to me when I worked for other companies. Even project partners you are working together with do it. I had a good working partner who would often urgently text me to alert me to urgent e-mails he had sent me. Double the urgency, half the fun. Any or all of these scenarios may happen to you on a daily basis. That's life in the workforce these days. Unfortunately, there is rarely the magic bullet solution that solves all problems, and these urgency filters won't eliminate these kinds of externally manufactured urgency problems. You can't control the actions of others all the time, but you can control how you *respond* (or maybe don't right away) to their manufactured urgency. At least, filters could eliminate the manufactured stress you and I may be nice enough to create for ourselves.

In the first month of using urgency filters, I got mixed results. On the work front, the filters worked quite well. When I asked myself why I was setting deadlines, I realized that often I chose a particular deadline because it helped me feel like I was getting things done. Of course, getting things done is necessary. That's what my clients were paying me to do. That, of course, along with getting things done well and with high quality. At times, though, I had set target dates for myself that were well beyond the call of duty when compared to the real deadlines. In other words, in my desire for urgency, I was expediting timetables in an unhealthy way. My urgency clock was not set at *reasonable*. It was set at *stupefying*. When I asked the urgency filter questions, in many cases, there wasn't a true business need for that urgent deadline. Sometimes, I chose urgency to show a client that I could drive results for them quickly or to show value to the company. I did that frequently for new clients as I tried to validate quickly that they made a good decision bringing me onboard to help them. Sometimes, I was just being a little competitive— which I didn't think was my nature but apparently is in me, even if buried deep down in my subconscious. After all, I wasn't running a business to fail. As I continued to practice using my urgency filters at work, I got better at setting reasonable deadlines, while also postponing some work simply by accepting that it wasn't even close to urgent. Surprisingly, my clients didn't even notice my change because the urgency I had created for myself was far more urgent than their needs had been in the first place. It had been entirely self-imposed in many cases. If I needed any

validation that this was the right approach, the radio silence from clients was it.

That's not to say that time-sensitive issues don't pop up on the business front. Business wouldn't be business if that didn't happen. There will always be last-minute challenges that come up, changes that happen with little time, or unanticipated needs requiring quick turnarounds. The percentage of tasks that fall into that category, though, is far smaller than before I started defining urgency in this new way. And the greatest benefit: my work stress dropped significantly. In turn, I stopped carrying that self-inflicted stress home to the family.

On the life side, reducing urgency proved to be much harder, and I wasn't as successful initially. I had a very hard time applying the filter of health and sickness as the only determinant of urgency. The bad news was that I continued to act with urgency on a few things that I knew weren't truly urgent. The good news was that more frequently I could ask myself why I had imposed a certain deadline on a family task—in particular booking family vacations, weekend excursions, or outings or purchasing something that we needed—which helped me realize that I could avoid unnecessary heartburn by postponing those things until the following week.

At the very minimum, my decreased urgency at work created a positive cascading impact on the life side of the equation by eliminating unnecessary stress. I didn't have to carry that around with me when I was interacting with my wife, kids, extended family, and even the pets barking incessantly, eating stuff I'd rather they didn't, or just generally making a huge amount of noise. I found more humor at home. Ben chasing the dog around the backyard while the dog was chasing the rabbit around the backyard while the chickens squawked and tried to jump out of their coop to get in on the action was damn funny to watch. It used to piss me off. Using urgency filters had allowed me to find it funny again. I knew that our dog truly appreciated that I chastised her a little less when she barked at seven-year-old kids walking by our house as though intruders were coming to loot everything we owned.

Curbing the superhero syndrome

My urgency improvements translated well into curbing my superhero syndrome. The filters reduced my daily list, so I was left with fewer items to prioritize and make trade-offs for to get to my three mission critical things. Initially, it didn't feel good on the ego that I was doing less, from a quantitative perspective. I used to get eighteen things done. Now I was doing six things. Quantitatively, I was twelve items less awesome now. A 66 percent decrease in dad awesomeness. And who of us doesn't want to be awesome in the eyes of the people we love? Reducing that by two-thirds didn't feel as good as I had hoped it would, even though I understood the positive upside of it.

Despite my ego hits and my initial concerns about the trade-offs, my business continued to run well. That might be an essential takeaway here for you: my ego may have been more responsible for the superhero syndrome than anything else. My ego may have been driving me hard as opposed to actual business requirements. I'm not a psychologist, so I won't venture into anything about any of your egos other than to say that it's worth a check for yourselves. As I often talk about with the leaders who I coach, it is important to ask yourself why you are doing the things you are doing. Once I understood my ego's role, I was able to do the formerly unthinkable: I turned down some new client work. That would have been blasphemy before any of this. Of course, I tried to be smart about it. Instead of closing doors, I looked for ways to keep those conversations going so that the business opportunity was still alive for another time. I struggled with a few cases where it was an opportunity that wasn't going to come back. I had to learn to be okay with that, which might have been the hardest part of this entire quest so far. I worried about the revenue loss while lying in bed at night. My pressures as the sole financial provider were still significant, but I needed to realize that I wasn't going to kill my business. It would just be a different business. I was changing it to allow for the work-life balance I had envisioned. And if my income stream took a hit, I had to be prepared for the fact that I couldn't do it all, as long as I remembered my bottom-end thresholds as defined in my work-life vision. As long as I maintained that minimum income level, I could work through this business change.

On the life side, things started to improve, even though I experienced some initial problems adhering to my life urgency filters. It took a few months, but I stopped doing crazy things like finishing a presentation for work at midnight so that I could accommodate driving an hour and a half in traffic to and from a full-day volleyball tournament. I allowed myself to be okay with missing some games so that I could finish work outputs at a time of day when most people were still awake.

I'll be honest: I still had days when I wanted to pile on the list. I still had times where I fell off the wagon. If you suffer from the superhero syndrome, you will too. The role of urgent superhero was a twenty-year habit for me and might be something you've had for a long time as well. As you try to curb it, recognize that it likely won't happen in just a few months as I had unrealistically expected that it would for me. Your job isn't static and easy to maneuver. Jobs have changing needs. Sometimes, they change quickly. You've still got family needs that probably never stop piling up. I still had a family with a baby, toddler, and teenager in the house. Sometimes, the family combined with the business was still a powder keg sending me to my closet in search of my superhero cape amidst a sea of wrinkle-free business shirts because so much was happening. You might be scouring your closet for yours too.

With that, here's another CAUTION: MISTAKES AHEAD issuance. I've lost track of how many of those I'm issued so far. As always, I show you these failures so you don't have to make them yourself. My journey to reconcile my work-life balance wasn't smooth and without bumps in the road. Here's an example of completely falling off the wagon on the superhero front. A couple of months into implementing the rule of three mission critical things, my wife and I ended up on a used car buying mission for Gabe. Ivan, Ben, Gabe, Jen, our thirteen-year-old niece (who had been staying with us for the weekend), and I crammed into our car and drove forty miles to meet a sketchy guy who was selling his sketchy 2001 Honda CRV on Craig's List. This all happened while I was concurrently preparing for a three-day working session for one of my clients that was going to start two days later.

The road trip started with our usual family circus tricks, most aptly defined by me trying to order drive-through at El Pollo Loco with Ivan crying to be fed, Ben chanting, "black beans, black beans, black beans, black beans, black beans . . ." from the backseat, Gabe texting the sketchy guy, my niece listening to Taylor Swift on her phone with her earbuds at a volume that was so loud she had to yell to let us know how crammed she felt in the backseat, all while my wife tried to convey to me everyone's orders and interjecting her desire to make sure that I ordered four different kinds of salsas. I was sure the El Pollo Loco employee was ready to call the police to let them know we were under the influence of something, driving around for our chicken fix.

If the journey started out comically, it finished sadly. The used car buying expedition ended with confirmation of our gut feeling that something was wrong with this car deal, and that something was sketchy about the guy selling it to us. We plowed through and got it done anyway, even though we knew we shouldn't have. The car purchase was on a to-do list, which had clearly violated the rule of three mission critical things, but we made it happen anyway.

After an exceedingly long day, we arrived home quite late. Instead of going to sleep, I crammed in my last preparation needs for my upcoming client meeting. I somehow managed to do a good job with my client session during the week, but the car we bought from a guy none of us hoped to ever see again ended up being barely functional at best, that is unless you liked trying to turn a steering wheel in a car that perpetually leaked power-steering fluid. As we always did, we found a way to solve the shoddy car problem, but it was another thing to solve that never would have been there in the first place had I not regressed into superhero mode.

Why do I confess my absurd used car buying expedition to you? I confessed Poopgate, so not much could be worse, I guess. The reason for the confession is to demonstrate how things can fall apart quickly when you let yourself regress. The tendency to regress into work-life superhero mode is going to happen when things get stressful because your energy is going towards solving the thing that is stressing you out as opposed to regulating your superhero habit. That is exactly how "Honda CRVgate" happened. Life got stressful. I got the superhero cape back out without even thinking about it. Old habits die hard.

The good news for me was that I started to regularly invoke the memory of that ill-fated and completely avoidable used car buying experience to discourage similar kinds of missions. Such missions used to be a regular part of my circus life. Now something interesting was happening when I put too many items on the list or tried another flawed maneuver like the Honda CRV debacle. Just looking at a long list made me pause. Sometimes it even gave me a low-grade headache. Before I started this change in my approach to work and life, the opposite had happened. If I had only a few things on the day's list, I felt compelled to add more. And I always did. If I did some crazy Honda CRV-like stunt, I would have congratulated myself for pulling it off, even though I was totally wiped out. Now, if more than three to five things show up on my list, I instantly try to figure out which could move to another day. Let me be clear: this isn't about becoming a procrastinator. The conscious act of shifting to-dos to other days is just a way to normalize an acceptable number of accomplishments on any given day to support a healthy, happy work-life balance. Again, it comes back to trade-offs.

After a few months, my perspective on the right amount to take on every day changed. And now I felt undivided, which allowed me to enjoy the things I was doing. The benefits of not feeling destroyed at the end of the day and being able to enjoy the fewer things I was doing turned out to far outweigh the downside trade-offs. And not feeling destroyed all the time meant I had a little reserve for those times when there really was a need for a work-life superhero. Then I actually had the energy to pull off the necessary heroics. This was a turning point in my search for work-life balance because for the first time in a long time, I felt like things were improving.

Eliminating the "Blend":
The Trap of Undefined Boundaries

Undefined boundaries make it easy for work to bleed into life and life to bleed into work, leaving you feeling scattered and unbalanced.

The next trap to solve was the "blend" issue—that mind-fracturing phenomena where one minute you are in work mode only to shift to life mode and then back again. Focusing on the mission critical things and managing urgency had certainly reduced my daily to-do list but hadn't eliminated the blend issue. This constant bouncing back and forth felt chaotic, fragmented, and reactive. Just when I'd be getting some momentum on one task in the work or life categories, I'd have to make a 180-degree mental shift into a different area of work or life. Sometimes, the shifting converged into trying to do a work thing while in the middle of a life thing or vice versa. There's a toll from all of that bouncing back and forth, and it isn't just the potential of a mental collapse. Bringing it back to the work I did with my clients, ultimately it comes down to productivity, effectiveness, and efficiency. If you are constantly bouncing around and not able to maintain continuity of thought or work, are things getting done effectively and efficiently?

At the beginning of my search for the holy grail of work-life balance, I frequently heard and read that there was less and less separation between work and life these days . . . and that we just needed to accept that. Big, well-known companies were even embracing this notion of work-life blend and building it into their cultures. I have a friend whose company even used work-life blend as a selling point during the recruiting process to show their forward thinking and progressive culture. Break the traditional boundaries. Bring your life to work. Or bring your work home. The dog could come to the office. The kids could come to the office, too, after school, as long as they were quiet while you took your conference call. You could use your cell phone for work and personal purposes, as long as you weren't doing weird stuff on social media. The question is what role technology plays in all of this. Is technology at the core of not only how we got to work-life blend but also why many of us seem to feel like work-life blend is the inevitable and only option we have for dealing with work and life balance challenges? It might be, but maybe not.

With technology, we are more connected now than ever, and that technology is indifferent to work or life. It doesn't care. It just provides a vehicle for us to connect. Connection sounds cool, but cool can have a downside too. That ubiquitous connectivity via the cell phone is very convenient. But is it so convenient that it becomes disruptive and even a distraction at times? All I had to do was remember my day-in-the-life and add up how frequently I wanted to, and did, check work e-mail on my phone while at Ben's speech therapy, physical therapy, and swimming lessons or Gabe's volleyball game, or while driving from one place to another (or while sitting in the bathroom). Back in our dads' era, there were natural boundaries. You couldn't blend work and life easily because you couldn't carry a phone around with you. You *had* to separate them because you weren't always accessible. That inevitably created its own kinds of work-life stress. Maybe *lack* of connectivity back then created the same kinds of stress for our dads that overconnectivity is creating for us. But for those of us now, technology has erased boundaries, for better and for worse. With the ability to connect all the time, the number of things coming at you—or even being initiated by you—are significantly greater than when those old boundaries existed. And those things come at you in real time. For me, it was a text from my mom while in the middle of a client meeting. A call from a client in the middle of playing at the park with Ben or driving around with Gabe. That urgent text from my business partner notifying me that he had sent me an urgent e-mail. Even if you don't take the texts or calls, research has shown that the beeping from your phone alone creates its own stress.[1] And if that doesn't give you stress, at the very least it distracts you—even if for a second— and fragments your mind temporarily and makes you less productive and effective at whatever you were doing at that moment.[2] Sometimes,

---

1   Sammy Caiola, "Phone Noises, Notifications, Are Stressing You Out—But So Is Silence," *Chicago Tribune*, April 24, 2017, http://www.chicagotribune.com/lifestyles/health/ct-phone-ringing-anxiety-20170424-story.html

2   Adrian F. Ward, Kristen Duke, Ayelet Gneezy, and Maarten W. Bos, "Brain Drain: The Mere Presence of One's Own Smartphone Reduces Available Cognitive Capacity," *Journal of the Association for Consumer Research* 2, no. 2 (April 2017), https://www.journals.uchicago.edu/doi/abs/10.1086/691462.

you succumb to texting back. Our technology allows everything to happen all at once. You can always be reached. On a recent vacation, I found myself saying: "I just need to take this one call . . ." This quickly became a slippery slope to something worse: "I just need to send out this one document . . ." This led me to falling all the way down the hill to search for the FedEx Office on a deserted island paradise.

Embarrassingly, I checked my e-mail while on something as sacred as paternity leave for Ivan, which resulted in clients sending me more messages, despite the fact that everyone knew I was supposed to be detached from work. And, of course, I told myself "this will take only a minute . . ." more times than I would have liked and even read work e-mail while bottle-feeding Ivan. Why did I do it? Rationalizing was easy. I needed to take these calls because my clients paid the bills around here, and I felt as though I couldn't risk turning the business off or drawing a line in the sand for even a few weeks of no accessibility. This business was my livelihood, and lots of dependents counted on me (even if one of them was a garage-plundering rabbit). Similarly, one of the leaders I coach recently lamented that he spent a good portion of his long overdue Hawaiian family vacation dealing with urgent company legal issues because he had made himself accessible and then couldn't get out of the rabbit hole. When I asked him why he did this, he didn't suggest that it was because technology had made him so accessible (even though it had). He said that his main reason was that he was worried that things would fall apart while he was away and that he would be held responsible. Technology allowed him to dial back in and succumb to his concerns and fears the same way it did for me while on paternity leave.

So why do we "blend"? Going back to symptoms versus root causes, technology is certainly an enabler but may be only a symptom of our lack of boundaries—a big, gnarly symptom. This question may get to the root cause:

Why do we fear reestablishing some hard boundaries between work and life that technology has erased?

With no disrespect to our dads' generation, our lives are harder in a different way. In that era, few people feared negative reprisals from boundary setting because everyone was already living with boundaries. Now, when fewer or no boundaries exist, you are confronted with the potentially negative perception of being someone who draws lines when no one else does. The bottom line is that few of us—myself included— redraw those boundaries because we fear the negative impact on our jobs. We don't want to kill our careers. We don't want to be "that guy" who gets talked about in the succession planning meeting as the employee who goes home at 5:00 p.m. and can't be reached after that. In my case, I didn't want my clients feeling like I wasn't reachable whenever they had a business need. Lack of boundaries may be a complicated problem that technology has exacerbated in a very big way.

In addition to what I just described, lack of boundaries also turns many of us into multitaskers, which gets into the business issue I described earlier around productivity and effectiveness. I personally had tried to take multitasking to an unprecedented level. Multitasking was my norm. I had been parallel pathing work and life for a long time— and technology had enabled me to do it. Signing Gabe up online for an SAT prep course while participating on a conference call. Texting Jen about the grocery list in the one minute I had between meetings. Taking a client call while at Costco, distracting me enough to inadvertently drive my shopping cart into someone else's. Well, at least it wasn't a car, but it was embarrassing. Of course, when I looked up, it appeared as though everyone else at Costco was on a call of some sort or another and texting too. It seemed like everyone I knew was living this technology-driven, multitasking, boundaryless frenzy.

Many of us have become accidental work-life blenders without ever having intended to do so. Or because we aren't comfortable drawing the lines necessary to exit the work-life blend. Picture a Venn diagram—a tool we use frequently in the business world to visually show commonalities and shared ground. It looks like two separate circles that overlap in the middle for things that are supposed to be shared between them. If one circle represents work and the other represents life, my Venn diagram would have looked like two circles almost right on top of each other with the shared middle representing 90 percent of the diagram. In the work-life blend scenario, many of your Venn diagrams might look strikingly similar. Many of my Vortex days were the result of this unintended lifestyle. It wasn't working for me; I needed to figure out how to establish boundaries in an amorphous world of technology that is built upon a foundation of *eliminating* boundaries, while at the same time not drawing such a hard line that I killed my career and livelihood.

The result of this prevalent work-life blend is that most of us never check out (or do it much less frequently than we should). It comes down to a difficult decision. An uber-connected world doesn't naturally facilitate checking out. You may have to find a way to manually reestablish boundaries for yourself if boundaries are essential to achieving your work-life balance vision.

Solution: Uncompromising and ruthless compartmentalization and line drawing

I conducted more research, this time on multitasking. I wanted to know how detrimental this habit was. The research and science basically validated what many of us already know—multitasking is a fallacy that technology makes us think is real and thus encourages us to keep multitasking. I read a study from Earl Miller, a professor of neuroscience at MIT—which made him a lot smarter than me—where he distilled the problem down to:

"Switching from task to task, you think you're actually paying attention to everything around you at the same time. But you're actually not."[3]

Instead of doing things simultaneously as the term suggests, multitasking bounces your attention from task to task at high speed. This is apparently bad for our brains and something we aren't even biologically hardwired to do. No wonder it feels so bad.

As I read more, I found that all sorts of experiments had been done on the subject, and all yielded the same results. Multitasking worsens your

---

3   Jon Hamilton, "Think You're Multitasking? Think Again," *National Public Radio*, October 2, 2008, https://www.npr.org/templates/story/story.php?storyId=95256794?story-Id=95256794.

outcomes and slows you by as much as 40 percent because your brain is stressing to work in a way that directly violates how it is biologically constructed.[4] There was that productivity and effectiveness result that I had intuitively thought was a problem. One study also showed that regular multitaskers had lower gray matter density in the area of the brain that handles empathy and emotional and cognitive control.[5] I hadn't been the best science student, but I did remember that our brain's gray matter was pretty important in separating us from chipmunks. The brain science confirmed my suspicion: we don't perform well when we bounce around, *and* multitasking contributes to our stress. Maybe that's why I frequently felt like I hadn't done as good of a job as I wanted to at work or at home.

All of this combined information led me towards compartmentalization. In the previous chapter, we focused on ruthless prioritization to identify our mission critical things and escape the superhero syndrome. What we are talking about now is ruthless boundary setting and line drawing. In my work-life balance journey, I took it to an extreme at first. Work time would be for work and work things only. Life time would be for life and life things only. I needed something that cut-and-dry. You may not. I decided to implement a rigorous schedule each week that was designed for compartmentalization. On my work days, I would get up at 5:00 a.m. and happily work like a dog until 8:00 p.m. I'd crank out as much work as I could without distraction from life—unless, of course, something passed through the life urgency filter. And on days focused on life, I would draw a line and ensure that work was not allowed to penetrate. If this succeeded, I theorized that I would essentially eliminate my habit of trying to multitask between work and life. That would be great if I could pull it off. Of course, this took me right back to the fear of checking out. How would my clients respond? I wondered if they would be flexible or if they would find problems in not being able to access me when they wanted to. How would my family respond? It seemed like the life side would be the easier part of the equation, but I wasn't sure. Taking such a bold, black-and-white stance in a world that was becoming more and

4   "Multitasking: Switching Costs," American Psychological Association, March 20, 2006, http://www.apa.org/research/action/multitask.aspx.

5   University of Sussex, "Brain Scans Reveal 'Gray Matter' Differences in Media Multitaskers," *EurekAlert!*, September 24, 2014, https://www.eurekalert.org/pub_releases/2014-09/uos-bsr092314.php.

more gray might be fraught with challenges. My clients couldn't feel like my work was compromised on their end, and my family couldn't feel like work was turning me into an absentee husband and dad (even though on selected days it was designed to do just that).

With compartmentalization, my fully dedicated work days needed to be well-oiled machines so that I could crank out a ton of work and free me up to have my fully dedicated life days. Therefore, I needed to be as efficient as possible while at work. Based on my convincing research, I recognized that I needed to also eliminate my perceived need to multitask *while at work*. Forget about the broader picture of work and life for a minute. I needed to apply compartmentalization to my dedicated work days, too, so I could consistently get everything done that work required and reduce the risk of work spillover into life days. Consider this for yourselves as well. If you have a multitasking habit at work (like most of us do), you might be less productive and efficient than you think you are, which in turn might cause you to break boundaries you were trying to set *between* work and home because things spill over when you don't get them completed by the end of the workday.

Small steps to reduce multitasking at work

To reduce work multitasking, I decided to take three steps. Like many things, they are easy to read about; they are harder to do with consistency.

1. **Eliminate distractions that encourage multitasking at work.**

   It is easy to bounce from task to task when you have your e-mail open, your cell phone nearby, and various other temptations vying for your attention. There was no question I needed to eliminate distractions. When I was on conference calls, I decided to close my computer or only open the file that was directly related to the call. If I was working on a presentation, I closed my e-mail. It is far too easy to lose track of what anyone is saying in a meeting while also responding to e-mails. Though turning off your cell phone might help with focusing on single tasks, most of us still need to keep it on in case of a family emergency. As a compromise, I turned my phone over and put it on the shelf instead of having it right next to my computer.

2. Make a to-do list of single tasks.

With distractions minimized, I could block time for single tasks without anything else taking that space. Experts have a name for this: "single-tasking."[6] What they mean is if you have ten things to do, schedule specific time for each individual task and focus only on that task during that block of time. This approach felt good to me since I was a terrible multitasker in the first place, even though I did it all the time. I had a feeling that I would get my work done faster when I wasn't trying to juggle. I hoped that I would get time back by completing single tasks faster, which in turn could allow me to get even more work tasks done, all in the name of having that clear conscience for "life" days.

3. Make "Be in the moment" a mantra.

Years ago, I worked for a company that had the mantra of "Be here now." I remembered thinking that it was cool but had never thought about how it related to multitasking. When you try to multitask, you aren't mentally invested in where you are at that moment because you are always bouncing back and forth. Forcing myself to be in the moment could reduce my inclination to multitask and couldn't do anything but improve the quality of my work since my mind would be completely focused on that task. This approach was going to take some time to get used to, though, because just like I had developed superhero and artificial urgency habits, I had also developed a multitasking habit.

Reigning in the cell phone

Next, I needed to figure out a plan for reigning in my cell phone use. I was checking it too many times during the day, even when I knew there was absolutely no reason to do so. And if I wasn't checking it, I was tempted to check it. I reflected on my day-in-the-life when I was plagued by a nagging itch to check my e-mail while stuck in rush hour traffic during my drive from that leadership meeting to Gabe's volleyball

---

6   Alina Selyukh, "Information Overload and the Tricky Art of Single-Tasking," *National Public Radio*, February 11, 2016, https://www.npr.org/sections/alltechconsid-ered/2016/02/11/466177618/information-overload-and-the-tricky-art-of-single-tasking.

tournament. If anything stuck in my mind about my cell phone, that was the image. I was a dad with a wife and four kids. Was catching up on work e-mails worth risking an accident for? I had to get this habit under control. So I came up with three simple rules (beyond actually obeying traffic laws about texting while driving). These were specific to my challenges; you may want to think about your specifics.

1. **No work cell phone while at the gym.** I was embarrassed that I needed this rule, but I did. It meant no checking e-mails while on the treadmill or elliptical machine, no work voice mail checks while doing bicep curls, and no "this will only be a quick call to this client" calls between sit-up sets. I felt better about the fact that I needed this rule after overhearing four conference calls that took place on the StairMaster machine right next to me in just one week. At least I wasn't alone.

2. **Cell phone stays off when with family.** No exceptions. Waiting in a long line would no longer constitute a legitimate excuse to check e-mail or send a quick work text.

3. **No cell phone for e-mail, texts, or anything else work related one hour before bed.** Checking my phone right before bed only sucked me into a rabbit hole and ensured I did not get a restful night's sleep, either because I ended up spending two more hours dealing with more e-mails or because the content of any of the e-mails upset me for a variety of reasons (as work e-mails tend to do).

These were my three cell phone rules. At first, they felt parental. I guess an interesting byproduct of this was that I now knew how Gabe felt when we gave him rules. I certainly felt that teenage desire to rebel against myself. But I was going to have to squash my rebellion if I wanted to give this compartmentalization strategy any chance of working.

Results and Outcomes—How did this all play out?

Life has an interesting way of surprising you. When I took on this strict compartmentalization, I would have laid down a sizeable bet in Vegas that any problems would have come from the work side. I would have lost a lot of money on that bet. Working with my clients to adhere to fairly strict compartmentalization was a lot easier than I had anticipated. I was sure that if I said I couldn't meet or call on a certain day, the client would be inflexible, and I'd have to invade the compartmentalized life time. Not so. Occasionally, a client might not have any other days or times or where a project required something to be done on a specific day. For the most part, though, my clients were as respectful of my schedule as I was of theirs. Compartmentalization on the work side was successful. Of course, it wasn't an instant flip of the switch where suddenly everything fell in place. I had my share of days where I had forgotten about a recurring weekly client call that was now scheduled on what was supposed to be a life day. For a few weeks, I scrambled around to deal with those memory omissions. All in all, though, work compartmentalization was effective. My business didn't fall apart. Clients didn't leave me. My fear of checking out was unfounded to a large degree. That might be the most important thing for you to take away. Checking out and drawing lines—if done with care, reason, some flexibility, and consideration for the needs of others—won't kill your career. Of course, running my own consulting business has inherent flexibility. I do have the ability to set my own calendar to some degree, as long as I stay on top of client needs.

What can you do to draw lines and set boundaries appropriately if you work for someone else? I cite a recent discussion I had with a big client of mine. As part of some project work I was doing for them, the company had a group of high-potential managers gathered in a forum to talk with top executives about whatever they wanted to talk about. It was designed to get out on the table the things these high-potential managers were most concerned about. The question of work-life balance and boundaries came up frequently—especially from those in the crowd who were parents. The answers the executives gave were revealing—even coming from leaders of a company that is about as hard-driving as they get. Essentially, the perspective of these leaders was that you have to draw your own boundaries because no company is going to do it for you . . . *or punish you for it if you do it with proper consideration.* To that end, none of the leaders—all of whom had kids of varying ages—said that going home at 5:00 p.m. to have dinner with their families several times a week, for example, had ever created any negative impact on their careers. Some even did weekly breakfasts at home and took their kids to school in the morning as part of their ruthless boundary setting. A few others talked about vacations being critical to creating complete separation from work. As one leader said, "Your job will be right there waiting for you when you come back." Her point was that you can check out and the world won't come to an end. Nor will your career. It was fascinating to listen to these perspectives and watch the managers start to recognize that boundary drawing was possible and could coexist with a very successful career. To that end, many companies are receptive to flexible work arrangements as long as the work gets done well and on time. Many of my own clients have those flexible arrangements in place.

Surprisingly for me, the difficulty with compartmentalization was on the life side of the equation. Maybe I had unrealistic expectations, or maybe I had temporarily forgotten that life with a wife, baby, toddler, teenager, neurotic dog, destructive rabbit, and eight chickens was so dynamic that something was always coming up. The bottom line was that for the first month of trying to have dedicated work days, not one of them actually played out like what I had envisioned. I had envisioned being an undistracted Robo-James, cranking out huge volumes of work to the point where word would get out to the business community and prompt random businesspeople to come by during their lunch hours just to marvel at my prodigious output and bemoan themselves as being "only human." In reality, what I lived was the need to take the dog for a walk and then do some work but also come home just a little early because Gabe had an after-school college preparation event for which we had promised he could use the car. Every supposedly compartmentalized work day was invaded with something or a few things or even a lot of things from my life side that might have been little things but in aggregate eroded any compartmentalization. The erosion of my compartmentalized work days in turn created the problem I had feared: work activities would then bleed into my life days since I couldn't crank out as much as I had hoped on my work days. Just one month in, the whole thing started to fall apart.

The question was whether compartmentalization was a great theory that had no business in reality or whether I wasn't managing it with enough rigor to make it work. This definite line drawn between work and life certainly was a different way of doing things than I had been used to. I called for a "do-over"—that childhood rule of forgiveness that allows you another chance at bat after you hit the ball into the neighbor's tree. Compartmentalization is hard. If you've tried it and failed, it deserves a do-over. None of us ever told the neighbor that the ball was in the tree anyway.

Some of my approach to unblending had worked well. I had done a good job with my multitasking rules and reigning in my cell phone. It was just a matter of getting the whole thing working. If I could figure out how to reign in the life part on those days when I needed full dedication to work, this approach could really work. My wife and I started having check-in meetings once a week to discuss the next week's work and family schedules. Together, we figured out which days I was going to be MIA around the house so that I could be fully present on the other days. Having a weekly business meeting with my wife felt a little weird, but it started to pay dividends. I can't take credit for the idea. It was hers. And it worked. I told her that she should be writing this book.

I also realized that you have to create a little flexibility around compartmentalization, without creating a slippery slope that leads you back into the boundaryless work-life blender. Some weeks, compartmentalization couldn't necessarily accommodate full work days. Instead, the workweek might be three full days and one-half day or three half days and a full day. And on some complex weeks, compartmentalization might mean life compartmentalization in the morning until 9:00 a.m. so we could have a family breakfast, work compartmentalization until 5:00 p.m., ending with life compartmentalization from then on so we could have a family dinner. Personally, those kinds of split compartmentalization days are my worst-case scenarios and not my preference. But after living a few of them, I realized that they still worked too. Regardless of which version of compartmentalization you end up with each week, it is important to always start from the place of full compartmentalization before dialing it back. I now always start from the place of several completely dedicated full workdays and work backwards to figure out the right thing for that week. What "full compartmentalization" looks like for you will be based on your work and life realities and will inevitably be unique to you. The point is to figure out what that looks like so you can adjust it as necessary to keep you out of the blend. I can attest to the fact that when compartmentalization works, it works *really* well. When it fires on all cylinders, I feel the best about both work and life balance. Life is always going to be dynamic, with unpredictable ups and downs, but at this point in my journey toward balance, I now felt like I had an approach that was flexible enough to accommodate unpredictability without abandoning compartmentalization. Now I was getting somewhere.

Cascading Positive Impacts:
The Trickle-Down Effect on Other Traps

By this point in my search for the holy grail of work-life balance, I was making some significant progress. Admittedly, there were no instant solutions. All of this progress had taken a few months and more trial and error than I had hoped and anticipated. But no one said it would be easy. I had a few battle scars. It was like I was learning how to ride a bike again but without the benefit of a helmet. My few bumps and scrapes didn't deter real progress on my end and should hopefully expedite your progress. As my dad used to tell me: "A smart man learns from his own mistakes. A brilliant man learns from the mistakes of others." I've made lots of mistakes on my work-life journey that you can learn from. If you are playing along in the home version of the game, here is where we are at this point:

- You have documented your day-in-the-life (mine will be forever remembered for Poopgate) as a way to capture your work-life current state and have pulled out three to four key observations and trends.

- You have developed an achievable vision for your work-life balance based on asking hard questions about trade-offs and priorities. For me, this was the first time in my life I had done that. A few elephants had officially left the room because of that.

- We have identified eight behavioral traps that are playing against attaining that vision. After taking a hard look at those traps for yourself, some of them may be more front and center for you. Or, if you are like me, there isn't enough front and center room on the stage because all eight are vying for the limelight.

- We have reconfigured the eight traps flowchart by grounding it in an understanding of root causes and symptoms, and we are able to start in the right place to make the most impact with solutions for each trap.

- We have solved for the trap of artificial urgency by implementing urgency filters based on criteria relevant to our individual lives.

- We have solved for the trap of the superhero syndrome by implementing the rule of three as a way of forcing ruthless prioritization and focusing on mission critical things.

- We have solved for the trap of undefined boundaries (and the related tendency to multitask) by implementing ruthless compartmentalization that allows enough flexibility to work in various job situations. We've also pressure-tested the potentially erroneous perception (but very real fear) that drawing lines and creating boundaries in a work environment will kill a career. We instead discovered that boundaries can be established if done with prudence, flexibility, and consideration for the needs of the business and the people with whom you work.

I was forming new habits and seeing positive results. When you get to this point in your path towards your own holy grail, you will likely be starting to see some progress around new habits as well. I was even feeling good enough to want to go find Darryl from AP and let him know that he wasn't the only dude who had figured work-life balance out, but I figured I'd let him focus on processing my invoice, which was now well past Net 30 terms. Maybe most importantly for me, at this point in the game, I now had a glimmer of hope that I wasn't doomed to an overwhelmed work-life blend after all.

The work wasn't done yet, though. The next test was finding out if efforts to eliminate the first three traps did indeed mitigate the traps of no buffer zone, constant triage, and chasing time. By virtue of the solutions implemented already, I was hypothesizing that I should be seeing positive signs in these areas, too, without even having tried to solve these next three traps yet. Regardless, each of these next three traps are obstacles in and of themselves and require individual attention. As usual, I'll describe them in the order that I addressed them—for better and for worse.

STARTING TO MITIGATE THE
IMBALANCED SYSTEM OF TRAPS

Solve the trap of the superhero syndrome by focusing only on mission critical things

Solve the trap of artificial urgency by using work and life urgency filters

Solve the trap of undefined boundaries by implementing strict compartmentalization

Would making big adjustments and solving for these three traps have a cascading positive impact on the other traps?

The trap of no buffer zone

The trap of constant triage

The trap of chasing time

The trap of late nights getting it all done

The trap of forgetting yourself

STARTING TO GET BETTER BALANCE

Building a Better Buffer Zone

No buffer means no room for error. Most of our lives don't work that smoothly. We need space to allow for the unanticipated.

The trap of no buffer zone had been a major challenge for me for a long time. I vividly remembered a conversation with an employee of mine earlier in my career. It was one of the first times I had people reporting to me, and I was relatively new with the company at the time. Sharon had been employed there for years and had a handle on how things worked there. I liked her. She was a hard worker and a good thinker. Our conversation came amidst a continually growing list of new projects to meet a continually growing list of company initiatives. The conversation was triggered when one of the big initiatives ran into some unforeseen problems causing a need for more resources—which we didn't have—resulting in the initiative taking longer to finish than anticipated. This then spilled over to our other projects that required the same limited resources and had deadlines that coincided with this project. In other words, we were a little bit screwed and had to figure out how to deal with too much work all needing to be done at the same time with not nearly enough resources. In *other* other words, we faced the typical business problem that seems to happen almost every day in almost every company everywhere. During my conversation with Sharon about how we were going to get it all done, she said something insightful: "We always make the same mistake. We only plan for the best-case scenario. We never think about what might go wrong or what might happen that we don't anticipate. When the unexpected does happen, we can't deal with it because there's no space to put it." At the time, I understood exactly how accurate her insight was. We were feeling the pain; we had to work harder, put in more hours, and cope with more stress to get the work done on time. On top of that, the extra work hours ate up time that should have been dedicated to our personal lives, making that time period feel incredibly unbalanced—and I wasn't even married yet, let alone a dad.

Looking back on that situation, I saw how frequently the company

didn't have any buffer zone in its planning. Lack of a buffer zone can be almost par for the course these days at work, and many of us have gotten begrudgingly used to it at work. As we learned from the trap of artificial urgency, it is easy for habits to spill over from work into our personal lives. My Poopgate day-in-the-life proved that. The entire day from start to finish had been one big buffer zone violation. I had left no room for error at all, and when errors hit in the form of a swimming pool poop debacle and a client meeting running late, the day went off the rails. And my stress level went off the rails with it.

So now came the time to look for evidence that things were different based on the three traps I had already worked hard to mitigate. For buffer zone violations, there's nothing more tangible than your calendar. It will show you—without compassion or commentary—just how much buffer zone you have or don't have. I chose to do a before-and-after comparison of snapshot weeks of my calendar. I chose one week from Sunday to Saturday from before I had started to make changes in my approach to the traps of the superhero syndrome, artificial urgency, and undefined boundaries. Then I chose a current week in my calendar (now several months into my work-life transformation) for comparison. You don't have to do the same comparison I did, but if you are looking to see if the changes you've already made are having an impact, this is as easy a way to do it as any. When I looked at my "before" calendar, which was from what I now call the "Vortex Period" of my life, two observations jumped out:

1. **There was too much stuff on my calendar each day.** I kind of expected to see that.

2. **There was no space between the too many things.** I kind of expected that too. I had frequently found myself squeezing meetings into any white space I could find. The activities I had for the life side showed the same problem. And when I had a work obligation right before a life obligation, I had left minimal time between those too. It was one thing to have back-to-back meetings where you don't give yourself the five minutes to walk from one end of the building to the next. It was another thing to have a work meeting end at 5:00 p.m. followed by a personal commitment at

5:30, without considering that the only way to make it there within that thirty-minute window was to magically fly there in your car, jumping over the gridlock on the highway, which you know exists every day without fail but somehow expected to miraculously vanish that day because you have a personal need.

When I checked my current calendar for comparison, there was noticeable improvement. There was more open space because I had ruthlessly prioritized what needed to be done. My trap solutions were working, and I wasn't delusional to try them.

This was all good news, and there was a little part of me that wanted to claim victory over the no buffer zone trap and move on. But I had fallen off the work-life balance improvement bike enough times in my journey that I knew better than to just move on, even though my calendar had buffer space between obligations. Falling on my head several times had definitely made me smarter this time around.

Some additional tendencies that create buffer zone violations still needed attention. I went back to root cause analysis. What were the root causes of buffer zone violations time and time again? The other traps we've already worked through were clearly part of the root cause, but so was a lack of buffer zones. I realized that this is one of those multivariate situations (if I remember my statistics correctly, which I often don't). There are multiple factors contributing to an outcome. As you think about buffer zones, beyond taking on too much, there are two additional culprits that create the no buffer problem:

1. **Underestimating how long tasks really take to complete (either because we are just impatient or haven't been able to think through potential monkey wrenches that impact time) and then allocating time for those tasks based on the fastest route possible—for better or worse—because fastest is what you hope it will be.**

2. **Having a hard time saying "no" to new things that impact your calendar.**

I don't know where you landed on those two things, but it shouldn't come as any surprise that I was guilty as charged on both. I was getting better at saying "no" (another way of setting boundaries) by virtue of everything I had done on the path thus far, but the other problem was an issue that needed to be resolved.

Chronic underestimation of time isn't something to take lightly. If you always plot time requirements based on the fastest possible timeframe, you are destined to continue to run into trouble any time that fastest path doesn't happen because everything else after it would now be behind schedule. Being behind schedule was inherently stressful for me and is for many of us. And when we get behind, we attempt shortcuts to get back on track and reduce our stress. If we can't shortcut the tasks, they continue to mount on our shoulders. Neither work nor family activities benefit from shortcutting, and nothing benefits from more stuff piled on our shoulders. The quality of whatever you are doing suffers. Personal interactions suffer. Relationships suffer. The bottom line is that a straight line from one destination to the next isn't always a good path. Sometimes, a curved route is necessary and should be the planned route. Most of us get this conceptually, but when things start to pile up in real life, avoiding shortcuts with rigor and consistency becomes a lot harder.

Solution—Part 1: Simplify and reduce things that aren't truly required

This starts with making some hard simplification decisions. If you are going to reduce the potential for buffer zone violations, you have to reduce the number of elements in your life that can cause buffer zone violations. If the decisions you've had to make so far in the search for balance seemed hard, this is where they get really hard. They certainly did for me. On an everyday basis, even after finding solutions for the first three traps, I still had my life as I knew it. I still had to contend with eight chickens, a dog, a rabbit, a baby, a toddler, a high school student, a college student, and clients. All were part of the ecosystem my wife and I had designed, but with this many dependents, lots needed attention. That meant I felt tempted to squeeze time, be impatient about time requirements, and underestimate time required in a desperate hope to take care of everybody. Your life complexities will look different—unless you also have chickens, in which case we'll have what we frequently call in the business world an "offline conversation" about the ups and downs of life with chickens.

What do you eliminate? Like every other part of this process, it comes down to asking the right hard questions and then being able to live with your answers. For those questions, I again come back to the work I do with my clients when they are considering operational challenges related to limited resources for competing priorities—a situation almost all of us have had to deal with in our careers. The questions are pretty straightforward:

1. **What is truly necessary and required? In other words, what is a need?**

2. **What is nice to have? In other words, what is a want?**

The initial tendency will be to say that everything is truly required. Why else would you be doing it? That's the common conversation I have with some of my business clients. To be honest, I've given that answer many times myself. To make the questions have more impact, they need to be then anchored in something. That something is the strategic vision or future state. With my clients, it is about deciding what directly supports that vision and what may not (even though we want it to). For work-life balance, it is the same thing. So the next hard question is:

Out of everything you classified as "required," which of those things directly support your work-life balance vision? Which don't?

After asking that hard question enough times, you usually find some needs become downgraded to wants. Here is how those answers played out for my wife and me:

1. **The chickens needed to fly the coop and go back to the farm.** We had grown to love the chickens (well, to be fair, it was kind of love-hate for me), and they were great for Ben and would be equally great for little Ivan when he was big enough to chase after

them. One thing that Jen and I both valued was teaching children at a young age how to appreciate and respect animals. That's why we had the dog, the rabbit, and the chickens (even though Ted didn't respect much as he gnawed everything). Ben was remarkably gentle with and unafraid of animals. Our pets required work, though. At this point in time, they were work that we just couldn't support in a way that didn't negatively impact lots of things around our little ecosystem, and that had me feeling stress and pressure. It was a difficult decision; we needed to reduce the number of animals in our home, namely by eight. My wife searched diligently to find a suitable home for the eight chickens where they would be taken care of and could live meaningful chicken lives (whatever that means).

1. **I needed to reduce my prospective client list so I could focus on "the vital few."** Business development is a funny thing. You want to spread a wide net to give yourself the best chance of catching something. But you also don't want to do a lot of unnecessary work that doesn't yield anything. In line with my new work-life vision, I chose to cast a tighter net and to focus my efforts, especially since I had now put my business in sustainability mode.

I had made only two initial decisions towards simplification. Reducing the infrastructure that needed support—even if just in these two small areas—felt like it could make a big difference. The point here is that you don't have to do a major life overhaul. In fact, I would suggest not thinking about anything close to that. You really need to change only a few things to see big impact.

Solution—Part 2: Build 50 percent additional scheduled buffer space into everything

To address the chronic tendency to underestimate the time it takes to get things done, many of us need visual cues to stop ourselves from doing it. You can start simply by adding an additional 50 percent of time to every activity on your calendar. If you estimate an hour for something, put it in your calendar for an hour and a half. Given the aggregate changes you have made already, your calendar should have space for this extra time. Mine did. And if any particular obligation really took only the time without the 50 percent buffer, you get the additional time back to do something crazy like think or even relax . . . or try that power nap. However, if anything unforeseen happens, you won't lose your mind trying to adhere to an unrealistic schedule. This is just a minor tweak but one that can have a big impact.

Results and Outcomes—How did this all play out?

I haven't missed the chickens since they've been gone—and that wasn't only because I didn't have to hear them squawking before the sun came out. It was one less thing that needed attention (or eight things if we counted each chicken individually). It was one less thing that could create unforeseen problems. My wife missed the "farm fresh" backyard eggs and defiantly declared that she couldn't eat eggs from the store anymore, but we'd work through that downside. Casting a tighter net on prospective clients did exactly what I had hoped—it kept me focused on the business development that yielded outputs and gave me back time from the eliminated development that didn't yield as much.

I still have more work to do around work and life simplification to support my work-life vision. But I had made two small steps. What I have learned is that simplification needs to become a mindset instead of a point-in-time activity. It requires constant attention. It requires you to always keep an eye out for those things that aren't truly necessary and eliminate them piece by piece. Even when you've simplified, keep paying attention because it is easy for things to just sneak back into the equation somehow.

At the same time, I was practicing adding 50 percent additional time into tasks I scheduled. Admittedly, this might feel like a mind game to you. It felt like a bit of a mind game to me, but it did have positive results because it created actual space on my calendar. It was like setting your clocks ten minutes fast so that you aren't late. You know you set the clock fast, so when it reads 4:30, you know it's only 4:20, even though your intent was to make you believe that it was 4:30. Part of the mind game is ignoring the extra ten minutes that you really have. If you don't "forget," you're back to being late again. It's the same with the additional 50 percent buffer budget. I knew the mind game I was playing. My desire to sabotage my own mind game didn't last very long, though. Maybe it was because I had already started forming new habits to counter the other traps. Maybe I was getting used to the fact that screwing a little bit with my head was part of my journey to the holy grail. Whatever it was, I stopped trying to undo things that were working, this being one of them. I was creating more buffer space. The extra 50 percent worked extremely well. If a curveball came at me—which happened almost every day—my stress level didn't escalate like it used to. That might have been the biggest payoff. I felt more in control even when curveballs hit that were out of my control. And feeling more in control resulted in better balance because I wasn't trying to catch up from being behind anymore..

Triaging Your Way Out of Triage Mode

If you don't give yourself time to plan your work and life, you'll always be in firefighting mode, feeling unbalanced and not in control.

I was feeling pretty good about myself at this point. I was now four traps into my search for the holy grail, and the blur was starting to clear up. I had significantly fewer things to do because I was better at prioritizing mission critical things. I was better at not making everything urgent, and I was better at compartmentalizing. Those three improvements resulted in more space in my calendar, which allowed me to schedule buffer space between obligations. I took it a step further by simplifying aspects of my life based on what was truly required instead of only nice to have. And I did this simplification in line with my work-life vision, which further ratcheted down the number of unanticipated things that could introduce chaos into the balance. Now it was time to get out of constant firefighting and triage mode. You might think that by this point, the triage problem solves itself. Unfortunately, it didn't. If constant triage—or living in a reactive state—is a problem for you, here is why it won't go away on its own.

Getting out of triage mode fundamentally starts with not only time allocated for planning but also *how* you plan and *what you plan for*. Before fatherhood, I had always been a committed planner. You probably had a system of planning that worked for you too. It probably worked well. Mine did. And that was because we all learned how to plan for the lives we were living at that time. In our lives before fatherhood, the planning revolved primarily around us as individuals and our spouses. That planning approach allowed you to manage your day, your week, and your life in a way that made you feel in control. Because I had a rigorous planning process for just about everything, I felt very in control of what I was doing back then. In fact, I had everyone fooled about how nimble I was. People at work used to comment about how quick I was on my feet in meetings. If they had known what only my wife seemed to know—I wasn't quick on my feet at all. In fact, sometimes my brain froze, but no one ever knew it because I had contingency planned for every single possibility of what could have happened at that meeting. That planning made me look quicker on my feet and smarter than I really was, and I'm not embarrassed to admit that. If people still didn't believe me, all they needed to do was watch my initial paralyzed reaction to Poopgate. I hadn't been able to contingency plan for that one, and I was hardly nimble at the beginning of that triage. I was equally good about laying out my career and almost rigidly adhering to my long-term wealth building strategies.

If most of us were good at planning, why in dad life did we feel so reactive? We could blame reactive living on trying to do too many things, leaving no time for planning. I probably would have put most of the blame on that initially, before addressing the superhero and urgency traps. Before getting those under control, I used to do guerilla prep for business meetings on the way to the business meeting, guerilla prep for hard conversations with Gabe on the drive home from the business meeting, and guerilla prep with Jen about Ben's preschool as we drove to the preschool. But I now had solved the "too many things" problem as well as a few others. Yet life was still reactive; I still felt unbalanced at times. Why? I'm not going to win any award for innovative thinking here, but the cause of this reactive state is that which makes us dads in the first place: KIDS.

I love kids. You probably do too. That's why we have them. The kids in and of themselves aren't the problem, and no one should jump to the conclusion that I have any plans for auctioning any of mine off (even the teenagers). But as we all know, real challenges come with being a dad for one, two, or four kids at any age. You are put in a reactive state to deal with things kids do that even with the best planning you couldn't have seen coming. And once you get beyond one kid, the reactive effect isn't additive. It somehow morphs into a multiplier. Of course, on the work front, clients, customers, coworkers, and bosses all exist in a dynamic state too. But they always have, and we've always had to plan for that. The real change is the introduction of kids and their unpredictability that can wreak havoc on your ability to plan. The bottom line is that since becoming a dad, you may need to figure out how to:

1. **Devote time to formal planning**

2. **Make sure to include all aspects of your dad responsibilities into your planning**

Since becoming a dad, I had never revised my methodology for *how I planned, when I planned, and what I planned* to include family life. Until I got to this point in the work-life balance quest, I had been not-so-blissfully unaware of that problem. Now it was painfully obvious.

If you don't adjust your planning methodology to account for family life, your reactive state becomes your norm. If you have no time scheduled in your day to plan, everything by default becomes reactive, which feels stressful and won't result in your best outcomes. It also means that you will fight fires that probably could have been avoided in the first place, taking up more time in your day. All of this can then erode the good work you've already done on the first four traps. Because of my lack of planning, I also found that I wasn't anticipating business issues and situations the way I used to before becoming a dad over the last ten years. That scared me; failing to anticipate potential client issues, revenue pipeline challenges, or business landscape changes had tanked much bigger businesses than mine. Constant triage is a significant problem. If it is one of the traps from which you suffer, it won't go away on its own.

Solution—Part 1: Schedule planning time into your day every day

By now, I had more space in my calendar. Your calendar might look clearer too. You can use a small piece of that newly found buffer to insert planning time. Be careful not to use up your entire buffer because you'll end up right back with a hectic schedule, but you are now at a place where you can use a little of that buffer without detriment. If you do this right, you won't even need to use your thirty-minute detox time for anything other than clearing your head—if you had implemented that approach. I was banking on the old adage: "An hour on the front saves you two hours on the back." With no buffer zone, there was never an hour on the front so there were always two hours on the back, which created the inevitable reactive state. Now I had space for that hour on the front.

Solution—Part 2: Adjust and broaden your approach to work and life planning

Now that you have planning time, you need to formally add the family stuff into your planning "agenda." In ten years of being a parent, I had never done that. You would have thought I'd have figured that out by this point in my life. We are all entitled to a few blind spots. This was one of mine. My planning had always been about my career and short- and long-term financial matters. Sure, once I was married and became a parent, I broadened that thinking to include the *implications* of my career on the family—such as job location and the bigger financial numbers required to support a family of six: from daily/weekly/monthly dollars required for a more complicated home ecosystem, to 529 college savings, to retirement savings now that a significant amount of money was going into raising four kids. I was good at making those kinds of adjustments. Those are the adjustments that felt a lot like what I do at work in terms of overall budget planning responsibilities. Maybe that was why I was doing a decent job in the business world and with running my small business.

Beyond that, though, I had never adjusted my planning approach to include what was happening with the kids. My wife was clearly doing that, and our agreed upon roles and responsibilities in our house suggested that she take the lead there—at least at this point in our lives. But that didn't mean that I wasn't and shouldn't be a part of that. In some ways, it doesn't matter how you and your spouse have divided your family roles and responsibilities. The effects of not anticipating and planning for kid-related challenges, needs, and issues find a way into your work-life balance equation. Lack of planning can put you into family triage mode in ways you don't see coming. It did for me—often. If you are suffering from a similar blind spot, you might need to make the same mental mindset shift I did.

During your now regularly scheduled planning time, don't neglect building in agenda time for each kid and the things going on each week that need to be anticipated. Anticipate ten steps ahead based on their tactical weekly needs and challenges the same way that you do with your career planning, work challenges and situations, and family financial planning. My wife taught me the ten-step rule, and it works, even though I'm capable of anticipating only two steps ahead of what my kids might do. I'm a dad. I'm not as gifted as my wife in that area. Probably because of that, my wife and I introduced little lunch planning meetings a couple of days a week. Sometimes, those meetings were by phone if I was at a client's business. Sometimes, we got to do it in person while Ben and Ivan napped. It helped us collaboratively plan everything going on in our circus. You may not use the exact same approach, but it is the mindset change that is most important here. Without that, you'll be blindsided a lot, and being blindsided makes you reactive.

Results and Outcomes—How did all of this play out?

As I had expected, I now had time for planning every day. It was easy, almost too easy. I felt a little bit like a guy having a good day looking around the corner waiting to be mugged. I did have a few days where it wasn't possible to protect the planning time, but I wasn't having to regularly bump it off my calendar due to competing urgent priorities. In fact, I discovered that I didn't even need *daily* planning. Because the planning time was so focused and undistracted, I needed it only every few days. Life and work were still dynamic, but every few days was sufficient.

For work, I got into a good cadence of regularly strategizing about my business pipeline and clients. I even added a regular networking outreach plan, which I hadn't done in years. Staying on the radar of business contacts that I had solid relationships with was a critical part of business sustainability. In constant triage mode, networking was the first thing that had fallen off my list on the business side. I put it back on and sometimes even used my planning time to reach out to past and present contacts. All of this together had me feeling back in control of a business that I was consciously changing to accommodate important priorities on the life side. Before revising my planning approach, my stress had come from feeling like I didn't have both hands on the steering wheel to turn the business carefully and prudently. Now I did.

On the kid front, I've admitted that I'm not particularly great at thinking ten steps ahead, which is confusing to me because I have always been very good at that on the work front. I guess the skill set may not be directly transferable without some practice and attention, which might be the key to all of this work-life balance change. At the end of it all, making sustainable changes requires focus and practice to break old habits and maintain new ones. Over time, I'm getting better at it. I consider it all a bonus since I never did any of that before. I was also able to keep my twice weekly lunches with my wife. I might have enjoyed those the most out of anything I had done so far in my quest for the holy grail of work-life balance. The family and life planning was certainly solving the constant triage problem. It by no means completely eliminated the reactive life we lead dealing with the kids of all ages, and it won't for you either. But at least I felt more on top of it. And maybe the real benefit was getting to spend alone time with my wife without being distracted or running around before and after it.

Enjoying Time Instead of Chasing It

Find a way to keep your mind in the present so you can truly appreciate what you are doing for both work and life.

Now that I was this far into my work-life balance transformation, I could finally solve the trap of chasing time: the tendency to focus on what's next instead of being in the moment and appreciating what you are doing as you are doing it. Before my quest began, everything was getting done, but something important was always missing. I was completing a race every day instead of enjoying the day. I was recently talking with a dad who coaches youth basketball with me, and he described it in simple terms: "Everything just feels rushed all the time." Days fly by at a record pace. I would get up and then suddenly feel like it was time to go to bed. Some days, I didn't remember many moments of the day at all. I had days where I couldn't remember what I'd eaten for lunch, and everyone who knows me well knows that I love eating. I lost count of how many times I arrived somewhere—whether for work or for my personal life—and didn't remember the drive itself. It wasn't a problem of being on autopilot. I simply wasn't focusing on what was happening in the moment. Many of us aren't. While doing one thing, you are chasing the next thing in your mind. It happens all the time. For lack of a better term, I call it "chasing time"—thinking about something else (often the next thing you need to do) instead of what you are doing right now.

I had a huge problem with chasing time. It is a challenge that is at the core of work-life balance. Most of us work because we have to, of course. But most of us have chosen a career or job that we do like. If we are chasing time, we are reducing how much enjoyment we get out of our work. In some cases, that can even cause us to resent our jobs. On the life front, we have our family. If we chase time, we miss all of the little family moments that will never come back, because we're not paying attention. Most of us won't be around when time machines allow us to go back and see what we missed while preoccupied with the things we were going to do next.

Some chasing time can certainly be attributed to having a lot to

do. Being busy makes the day go fast. When you cross the line into superhero busy, your day happens in a blur. I recalled one day months back while playing with Ben—which is something I value more than almost anything else—I found myself thinking about the three e-mails I needed to send out, taking Gabe to a soccer game, and the report I had arbitrarily assigned to myself to get done that day. Then at Gabe's soccer game, I thought about when I could play with Ben again and other work projects. My mind-body separation occurred because I had put all of these things and more on my list for that day. I rushed to finish one obligation to make sure I had enough time to get to the next one while simultaneously thinking about the next few activities.

Even though we've hopefully by now negated many of the causes of an overly packed daily to-do list, you still have a list (albeit a much shorter one). It will always be necessary to stay on top of what needs to get done each day so that you can plan for the next day. But the trap of chasing time isn't really a *planning* issue. Chasing time is a mental habit, one that many of us have been doing for a good amount of time—years in my case. Just because you have fewer things to do doesn't guarantee that you will inevitably change where your head is. Though a shorter list can certainly help, really, this is a mental "time zone" problem. At this stage in the game, we can probably solve the time zone problem since other contributing factors have been mitigated. At this point in my own journey, I was ready to stop chasing time and knew it was necessary if I wanted to grab ahold of the holy grail of work-life balance I was so close to achieving.

If you suffer from a time zone problem, you have to reconcile when to spend time thinking about what is next and when to stay in the present moment. Thinking ahead, planning, being future-oriented, and anticipating what is coming are all important. They had played fundamental roles in my own business success. And not just in running my own small business. Every day at work, you are confronted with situations where seeing downstream effects and anticipating them helps you do your job better. Thinking about the next thing is actually a good habit. If we think back to the planning approaches that help mitigate the trap of constant triage, much of our success in life is based on thinking about the future and what is coming next and next after that. It is a good habit but only when done by choice and appropriately so that you don't miss out on the present moment and enjoying your work and life.

Solution: Commit to living in the moment

The solution comes down to this: keep your head in the present instead of mentally traveling to a future activity (even if that future activity is going to be awesome). When my lists were too long, I time traveled to the next several things to make sure I could get them all done. When my lists got shorter and more reasonable—which they now were most of the time—I still time traveled out of habit at the expense of enjoying the present. You have to constantly remind yourself to stay in the present moment. Out of everything we've talked about so far, this seems the simplest and most straightforward. Yet, it is actually the hardest thing to do. The experience I had trying to keep my body and mind in the same time zone shows how hard it is.

Results and Outcomes—How did this all play out?

Old habits die hard. With big events, it worked very well. On the family front, we took a big family trip to Disneyland, and my mind was entirely in the present. It was an awesome day. There was no "next thing" thinking going on there at all, other than what ride was going to blow Big Ben's mind next. Even months later, I remembered his excited face when he saw the big sun at the end of "It's A Small World." That day felt like it went slowly, and that was the best pace I could have asked for. People may say that time flies when you're having fun. The intent here is to find ways to slow the fun down to really enjoy it. On the work front, when I had a big team meeting to prepare for and lead, I was also good at staying in the moment, and that increased my satisfaction for my work and what I could do to help my clients.

As well as those examples played out, I still fell into "next thing" thinking when I was doing smaller tasks. Then I noticed a trend. The smaller and more informal the event was, the more likely I was to slip into "next thing" thinking. When I took Ben to the park for an hour of play time, when I was walking the dog, or when I was checking work e-mails, these were the moments I couldn't remember because my mind and body separated. Ironically, for many dads I talk to, these little moments are the moments that you really want to enjoy and appreciate the most. The lesson I learned was that keeping yourself in the present moment for big days and big events is easy because the events are big. They demand attention. Little events like trips to the park are the times when you have to prompt yourself to stay in the moment. Those are the moments you don't want to miss. They won't demand your attention, so you have to make an effort to be present and give them the attention they deserve. If I had to boil it down, that's probably what work-life balance was really all about for me.

Chasing time was unexpectedly the most difficult trap for me to break. I kept working at it, though, and it started to get better. When I practiced my solutions for the other traps, the greatest reward was that I could be right where I was. I worked as hard as possible every day to slow things down. I didn't want to rip through my day. I wanted the moments to last instead of flying by. That was the best motivator of all because when I did slow my mind down and kept it resident where it belonged—in the here and now—I found that I didn't have to think about work-life balance anymore; it was already being accomplished. I was thinking only about the activity I was doing. I just needed to make it happen with more regularity and more consistency. It just takes practice. And for me, because it was so easy to slip into "next thing" thinking during small events, I had to develop a mindset for keeping me in those moments. Maybe put more accurately, I needed to develop a mindset to catch me when I mentally departed from the activity I was doing. To be honest, I'm still only operating at about a 50 percent success rate, although at least I have successfully snapped out of thinking about work e-mails while taking Ivan for neighborhood walks in his stroller.

Dealing with Late Nights Getting It All Done

Sleep matters. Enough said.

Here's what I've learned in life. Some people are Republicans. Some are Democrats. Some people are Yankees fans. Some are Red Sox fans. Some people are dark chocolate people. Some are in the milk chocolate camp. And some people are morning people while some people are night people. In most of those examples, there are people in each camp who won't actually talk to people in the other camp. There's real animosity there. In the case of work-life balance, I'm advocating strongly for the morning camp, which will sound awesome to morning dads but could cause night dads to close this book and walk off. Hopefully not. Or at least hear me out first before you close the book and walk off.

The funny thing is that even though I'm a big proponent of getting up early, it isn't because I'm one of those people who magically wakes up at 5:00 every morning, jumping out of bed with shockingly unnatural levels of exuberance. We all know those people. I'm scared of those people. Quite the opposite is true for me. I often give my alarm the middle finger when it wakes me up. But there are some real advantages to getting up early, and I'll talk through them, as well as my own experience getting there. That being said, if you think it's all garbage and you like being a night owl, we can still be friends, and you can still have work-life balance. We might talk more trash to each other, but I think we can still work things out. Perhaps the key to night owling might be applying what I've learned about getting up early in reverse. That might make more sense as we go through it.

My quest for the holy grail of work-life balance felt a lot like riding a bike downhill by this point. The ride was getting easier and was now kind of enjoyable. It had taken a great deal of effort to climb the hill and make changes to the worst of my habits, but I was experiencing a shift away from a system of traps to a system of proactive guidelines and solutions that supported work-life balance in a sustainable way.

MOVING FROM A SYSTEM OF TRAPS
TO A SYSTEM OF PROACTIVE SOLUTIONS

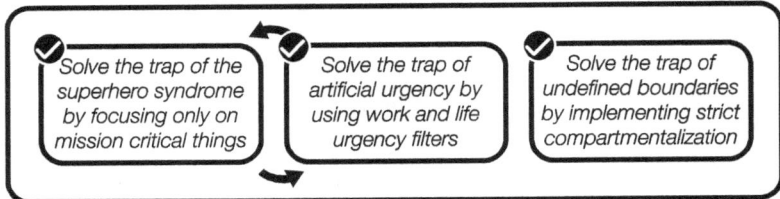

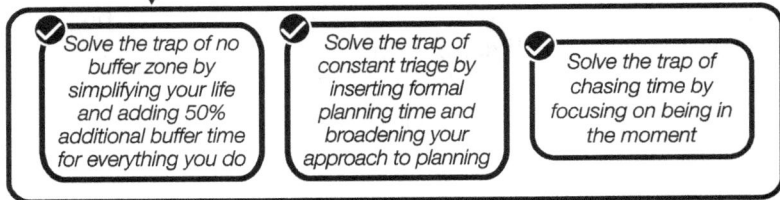

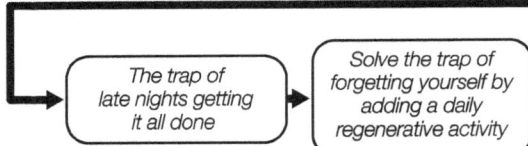

Solve the trap of the superhero syndrome by focusing only on mission critical things

Solve the trap of artificial urgency by using work and life urgency filters

Solve the trap of undefined boundaries by implementing strict compartmentalization

Solve the trap of no buffer zone by simplifying your life and adding 50% additional buffer time for everything you do

Solve the trap of constant triage by inserting formal planning time and broadening your approach to planning

Solve the trap of chasing time by focusing on being in the moment

The trap of late nights getting it all done

Solve the trap of forgetting yourself by adding a daily regenerative activity

Would it now be possible to eliminate long days and late nights and successfully insert myself back in the work-life balance equation?

STARTING TO GET BETTER BALANCE

Now I needed to address the hours I was keeping, in particular the trap of late nights getting it all done—the pressure of trying to finish things when I was already drained from a long day of work and life. Before launching my quest, I had felt as though I had no choice but to work late. You might have found yourself in the same predicament. There was just that much to do. If you were like me, it wasn't as though you were staying up late because you were sleeping in and shifting your whole day later because of personal preference. Some of you are truly into working late at night and have the job flexibility to wake up later the next day. But I've found that even if the job allows for that, my family life doesn't. Kids are up early. And if they aren't, they need to be, for school and other commitments which don't care that you were up late the night before.

The greatest cause of my late-night work hours was that the exceedingly long days didn't allow me enough time to get it all done by a more reasonable hour. Back before I had started this work-life quest, late nights used to pile onto early mornings. Now that my overpacked days were no longer overpacked, maybe I could finally eliminate those late-night work sessions.

As I have done before at different points in this journey, I will start with some interesting research; this time about sleep, staying up late, and getting up early. I found a number of interesting studies. Some show that getting up early correlates strongly with success. One study showed that getting up early correlated with higher GPAs for students.[7] I naively showed this one to Gabe and Dani thinking that empirical data would make an impact on them. Somehow, they found a way to completely rebuff this research as invalid, probably because it compromised their desire to stay up late and binge watch their favorite shows before getting to their homework at the last possible moment before their eyes closed on their own. Another study explains that you make fewer mistakes if you write in the morning versus burning the midnight oil.[8] That certainly explains why parts of this book needed a lot more editing than

7   Charlene Laino, "Early Birds Get Better Grades," *CBS News*, accessed June 19, 2018, https://www.cbsnews.com/news/early-birds-get-better-grades-09-06-2008/.
8   Karen Hertzberg, "The Early Bird Catches the Word: Analysis Shows We Write Better by Day," *Grammarly* (blog), last modified September 27, 2016, https://www.grammarly.com/blog/analysis-shows-we-write-better-day/.

other parts. I made a written apology to my editor about that one, and I made sure to write it in the morning. Even biologist Christoph Randler noted in his study that the physiological elements of getting up early could be strong drivers for school and career success.[9] Regardless of the studies, I know that there are a lot of dads out there who regularly pull off late nights and seem to still be surviving. I have friends that do it. It comes down to your work-life balance vision and how you have chosen to compartmentalize. I personally wanted to be involved with my kids in the morning. If I stayed up late, that was hard to do. I also know myself. My brain doesn't work properly past a certain hour in the day. Quite honestly, I say a lot of things that make no sense after about 10:30 p.m. These studies confirmed what I already felt personally. Getting up early, even if hard to do at times, got me better results and was better for me physically, emotionally, and intellectually. All of that, theoretically, should make me a better dad and a better businessman.

Then again, given how I grew up, how could I argue for late nights? I grew up in a house with a dad who was up every day like clockwork at 4:30 a.m., at the gym by 4:45 with his crazy morning cronies regardless of the weather, and at work by 5:30 a.m. He was an inspiring role model, whom I chose to emulate earlier in my life. For a good stretch, I was that same early morning madman and, with the exception of a few days here and there, had learned to love it.

The "day-in-the-life" business case for getting up early

Forget about the research studies for a minute. Here's my real day-in-the-life case for being up with the dawn patrol. For the first two decades of my career, I was up with the dawn patrol. Because of that, I was always ahead at work. I was rarely stressed. I had my career plan thought out and in place. I had time to plan my financial strategies. I sometimes ventured into crazy territory by going to the gym with my dad and his cronies. Even if I didn't, I was up going for a run and reveling in the fact that it was still dark and a bit cold, but I was out there getting it done while everyone else was still sleeping. I loved the old US Army

---

9   Christoph Randler, "Defend Your Research: The Early Bird Really Does Get the Worm," *Harvard Business Review*, July-August 2010, https://hbr.org/2010/07/defend-your-research-the-early-bird-really-does-get-the-worm.

commercials that proudly proclaimed: "We do more before 9:00 a.m. than most people do all day."

I wasn't the army, but I got a ton done before a lot of people were up and rolling, which helped me cruise through the rest of my day. Even before I started my own business, when I was working for various companies that had me attending back-to-back meetings from 8:00 a.m. to 5:00 p.m. every single day, I wasn't feeling the stress of mounting piles of work that I couldn't get to. As an introvert, despite the onslaught of all-day meetings where I had to talk to other people, my need for alone time was already fulfilled, before everyone else's day even started. Maybe coincidentally, work—even when it required extremely long hours at times—didn't feel that invasive to my personal life. I was up super early, which didn't always feel great at first, but I felt balanced.

Then Dad Life Happened

Then something happened. *Family life happened.* My wife and I had taken on "insta-parenting" responsibilities for Gabe and Dani, who were seven and eleven at the time they moved in with us. We went through a trial-by-fire approach to parenting an elementary-aged kid and a tweener, then a tweener and a teenager, and now a teenager and a young adult accompanied by a baby and a toddler. We did all of this while I took a big chance by leaving a successful and safe job working for companies for my own consulting business. And then, of course, rabbit, chickens, and dog. As family life got more and more involved, my energy and discipline started to fade. I lost focus and started sleeping in a little later each day. "Another five minutes won't kill anyone. Okay, let's give it ten . . . just today, though."

Then I started moving my alarm ahead instead of snoozing it several times. Who could blame me? I was *tired*. It wasn't like I was getting up at 10:00 a.m. on a workday and strolling in for a lunch meeting. But I wasn't getting up at 5:00 a.m. anymore either. What started as 5:15 a.m. "just this once" devolved into a new wake up time of 7:30. Getting up at 7:30 in the morning didn't put me in the category of lazy slob, but there was a marked difference between 5:00 a.m. and 7:30 a.m. in terms of just how little time I had to ease into my day the way I wanted to. When I got up at 5:00, it felt like a controlled slow roll where I could get things going at my own pace. At 7:30, I felt like I was getting shot out of a cannon into an action-packed circus that was already at full throttle and hitting on all cylinders. Then the pile-on effect happened. Because I couldn't knock out something for work in an hour before the house was up and running, I had to do it at 9:30 at night after Gabe's soccer practice when I was tired and slightly grumpy. Now, instead of cranking it out in an hour, it took me two hours. That alone increased my grumpiness level. I started at moderately grumpy simply because I was working at 9:30 p.m., but the fact that it took me until 11:30 p.m. to do something I knew used to take me half the time pushed me to grumpy old man status—and I wasn't even an old man yet, although I certainly felt like one by that point at night. I wasn't in control of my life anymore. My life was in control of me.

My nights didn't get longer because I had more to do. The nights got longer because I had more to do *coupled with the fact that tasks took longer to complete the later it got.* This meant that I couldn't get as much done that night, causing it to spill over to the next night. Because I had been up late the night before, I couldn't get up early the next morning. The work took longer, which created more late nights, which made the work take even longer, while I became more and more tired. It was the snowball effect I couldn't escape.

As my life demonstrates, late nights can cause you to get stuck in a reactive state. And that reactive state drives imbalance. I mention this because of one really important point. You don't want to inadvertently degrade any of the work-life improvements you have made so far by sliding back into a reactive state due to consistent late nights. Because of the positive changes I had made in the past months, I had the capacity to address my late-night rut and right the ship. Getting up early on a somewhat consistent basis could be the final piece in your search for the holy grail. I was highly motivated for early mornings at this juncture in my journey. If I had tried this sooner in the work-life transformation process, there was no way in hell I would have had any motivation to do it.

Solution: Introduce (or reintroduce) yourself to the dawn patrol and set cutoff points the night before you so can wake up early the next day.

This solution isn't complicated. You don't need to invent a new kind of math to solve this equation. The math already exists. I needed to recommit to rising at 5:00 a.m. again. You may not need to get up that early. Or maybe you need to get up earlier. It's about getting up early enough so that you can preempt the work-life challenges of your day. The key barrier to making that happen is the difficult challenge many of us face: going to bed at a decent hour the night before so that you can actually wake up early the following morning. And this is where many of us—myself included—fall apart quickly when work and family life come together. In my life, I had to realize that Gabe's after-dinner high school soccer practice, for example, wasn't going away until the season was over. Being actively involved in Gabe's teenage life was part of my work-life vision. I still couldn't quite believe that high school students had sports practice this late. I remembered what seemed like a simpler time when I played varsity basketball in high school. Our practices were from 2:30 to 4:30 every afternoon. The good old days of practicing when the sun was still out. I couldn't control Gabe's soccer practice time, but I could change what I did after Gabe's soccer practice ended at 9:00 p.m.

Whether you have to transport your kid to and from late-night soccer practice or have something else going on, it comes down to: *setting a cutoff point.* As I had slipped into more and more work-life imbalance, I realized that I had no cutoff point, not even an informal one that I continuously violated. A cutoff point hadn't crossed my mind, despite implementing technology cutoff points for the older kids at various stages of their lives. So what was my cutoff point after which I would not do any more work projects or e-mails? I decided that I needed to go right to bed after Gabe's practice (as well as accept the embarrassing fact that I went to bed only slightly later than my two-year-old). This isn't about putting something off until tomorrow. It's understanding that if you can get up early the next morning, you'll likely be able to get things done in half the time and with better quality.

Of course, as I had learned from the other trap solutions, habits are hard to break. An appropriate sleep schedule comes down to using willpower at first until it become the new habit. To get there, I considered putting a picture of my late dad next to my bed. He had somehow found the willpower to get up early almost until his dying day in his midseventies when he was already ravaged with multiple diseases. No wimping out allowed here. If my dad, otherwise known by his endearing nickname "Max the Axe," was able to get up early when he was in a dilapidated state late in his life, I could do this. I wasn't going to let the old man down. If I needed to invoke the memory of my late dad to pull this off, I was going to use it.

Results and Outcomes—How did this all play out?

Like almost everything else I had done in my search for the holy grail of work-life balance, for the first few weeks, it worked great. It was a reset of sorts, and I derived a lot of energy from it. Like most things, though, when you get beyond the honeymoon stage and realize that this new effort doesn't have an end date or a finish line to motivate yourself towards, it gets a lot harder. These days, when I have the willpower to get up early, I am grateful the entire day that I did. There are still moments early in the morning when I look at the clock, give it the middle finger, and go back to sleep. The habit of getting out of bed early is still being rebuilt. It's not as though I always loved getting up early, even before I was a dad. But most of the time, I knew that if I could get beyond that first unpleasant hour, the endorphin would kick in from the positive feeling that I was getting a whole lot done, taking care of my personal needs, getting my introvert quiet time, and everything else that seems to get put on the backburner once everyone is up.

Equally difficult is having the discipline to not get sucked into things late at night. There's always a reason to "just get on the computer for a few minutes." There's always an e-mail to send. There's always an article to write. There are always bills to pay. There's always work to do. I've resorted to physical prompts. After a certain time of the day, I put my laptop into my backpack. Get it out of sight. Remarkably, this has been working. Before starting this new trick, I probably still jumped on my computer about 50 percent of the time at night. Now I have to open my damn backpack and plug the thing in. It's not the most painful process to go through, but it's fascinating how just having to do that deters me from working late. Then I wake up fresh in the morning and crank through the work.

Here's the bottom line on getting up early. I don't do it every day. I don't want to do it every day. I probably won't ever do it every day. What I find is that when there is a lot going on—which still happens at times, even with all of the work-life changes I have made around the eight traps—that's the time to force myself to get up early. I'm not as regimented as the army, and you don't have to be either. Similar to the notion of flexible compartmentalization that we talked about earlier, you can implement the same flexible approach to getting up early. Do it selectively. Do it when it is necessary. That approach has worked perfectly on my end without making me feel like I now had to live a life where I could never sleep in past 4:30 in the morning.

Putting Yourself into Your Work-Life Equation . . . Again

After addressing the first seven traps, now you can go back and allocate time for your daily restorative activity. When I had tried it the first time, it had failed because I was implementing solutions in the wrong order. Now you have buffer time. Now you have priorities. Now your calendar has white space in it. With all of these improvements, there can be space for yourself. Space that was missing when I had tried before.

I went back to my three restorative activities—piano, gym, and *The Far Side*—and threw them back into the equation. I now play piano again. I don't play as often as the musician inside of me would like, but the realities of toddler and baby nap times do put some constraints on my desires to play at whatever time I now have space available. I am playing once a week. When I do play, it isn't for long spurts compared to my professional musician days when I could go for hours at a time. Nowadays, I put in maybe thirty to forty minutes at a time. But I am playing, and it feels awesome. That's what matters. A close second is that I have learned how to play well enough to be able to play that awesome blues riff Bill Murray's character showcases in the party scene towards the end of the movie *Groundhog Day*. My musical goals certainly aren't what they used to be, but that riff had always been my dream for my piano playing. That, and of course being able to play the *Peanuts* theme song for the kids. I'm not going to get picked up by a major record label with these piano selections (as were my aspirations back in the day when I was plugging my electric violin into a Marshall amp and trying to blow people's minds), but I'm having fun with the piano. That fun depends entirely on my ability to sustain everything I've done to overcome all of the traps outlined in this book.

I'm also working out at the gym three times a week. I get a solid hour in each time and don't feel rushed through it. I have been involved in sports my entire life and have missed the gym time, but not because I aspire to any athletic achievement like back in the day when I had a somewhat ridiculous goal of becoming the first Jewish guy with a forty-inch vertical leap. These days, just getting on the elliptical machine and doing weights on a regular basis is good enough. I just want to go out and shoot baskets without being sore for two weeks or get out and snowboard again.

I read *Far Side* cartoons too. I was able to cycle through the entire three-volume set of bizarre but hilarious cartoons. I've started to cycle through them again just for the hell of it and because I can. The cartoons don't get old.

Maybe most importantly, my wife and I are doing better at having lunch together with some regularity each week. Sometimes, we use them to plan. Sometimes, we use them to hang out. Sometimes, we use them to just rest. There are weeks where that time just doesn't materialize, and there are days when I can't do any of my restorative activities, but it isn't a chronic problem anymore. None of these things are falling off the cliff this time around. Now that the rest of the work-life balance system had been adjusted, I could put myself back in. So I did. If my experience is any barometer, you should have room for your own restorative activities too.

A SYSTEM OF PROACTIVE SOLUTIONS
TO ENABLE SUSTAINABLE WORK-LIFE BALANCE

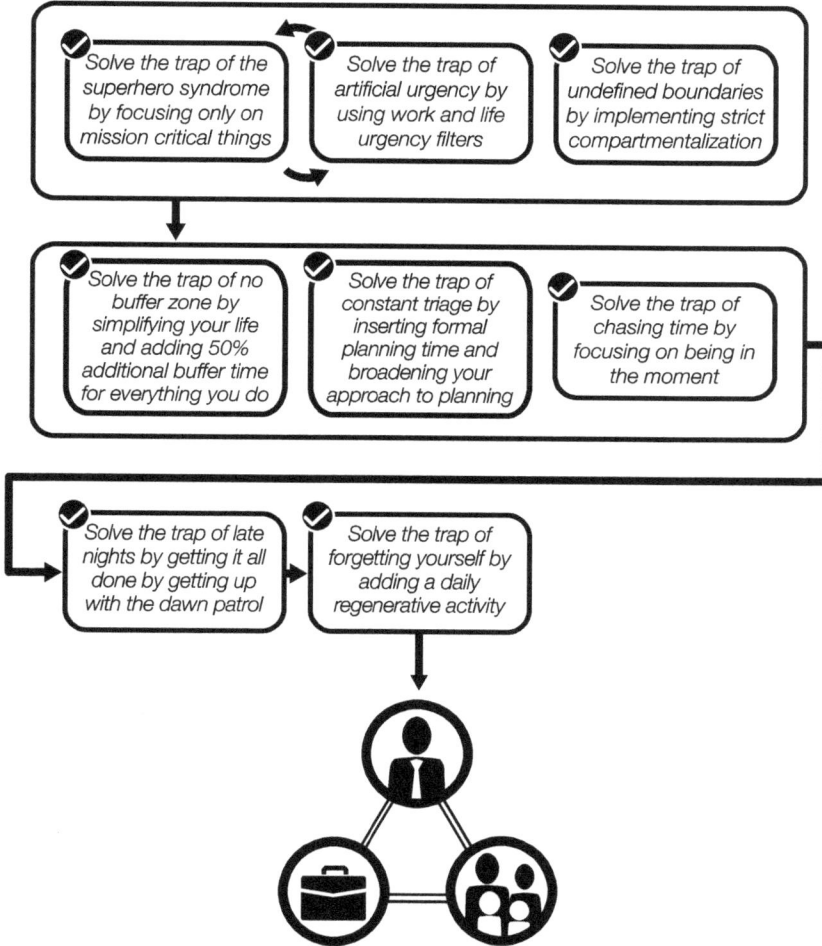

Solve the trap of the superhero syndrome by focusing only on mission critical things

Solve the trap of artificial urgency by using work and life urgency filters

Solve the trap of undefined boundaries by implementing strict compartmentalization

Solve the trap of no buffer zone by simplifying your life and adding 50% additional buffer time for everything you do

Solve the trap of constant triage by inserting formal planning time and broadening your approach to planning

Solve the trap of chasing time by focusing on being in the moment

Solve the trap of late nights by getting it all done by getting up with the dawn patrol

Solve the trap of forgetting yourself by adding a daily regenerative activity

A SUSTAINABLE HOLY GRAIL OF WORK-LIFE BALANCE

Part IV: What about That Holy Grail?

A Work-Life Balance Report Card

After all of this searching, did I find the holy grail of work-life balance? Close enough. I'm not in the Vortex anymore, and that's a giant step forward. Even though I had been dreaming of work-life balance for years, it had been only in the last year that I had gotten fed up enough to make that dream my new reality. Now almost a full year later, Ivan is almost a year old. Ben is three, successfully potty-trained, and talking everyone's head off incessantly like a little chatterbox (much to our relief). Gabe is seventeen and a junior in high school, driving around on his own and living his ever-evolving adolescent life towards independence, sometimes causing me huge stress and other times giving me great pride. Dani is still off in college making her way in the world. Jen and I are doing great. My business is still running. Sustainability mode certainly feels very different, but it is working. Life is certainly feeling better. At the same time, it's still challenging. A life with teenagers and toddlers is never going to be a cakewalk. Running a business is never something that can be phoned in. My search for the holy grail of work-life balance wasn't intended to solve those challenges, and it won't solve those kinds of challenges for you either. Those are the realities of our lives.

If I go beyond gut feel, how am I *really* doing? For that, I'll refer one last time to the work I do with my clients. In the business world where I spend a lot of my time, you rarely receive a bonus payout for *feeling* like you have done a good job. As part of my ability to evaluate if a situation has improved, I look for concrete differences between now and a year ago. Depending on where you are in your work-life balance journey, you may want to do the same thing. To do that, it is as simple as revisiting the work-life vision you created. If you want to take your evaluation a level deeper, you could document a day-in-the-life now and compare it to your first day-in-the-life. You can also monitor and evaluate yourself on how you are doing against the eight traps. I actually do this every day (my success with the traps varies depending on the day). Here's where we've landed on each of those:

1. **The trap of the superhero syndrome:** the detrimental effects of thinking you can do everything

Solutions: Ruthless prioritization and the rule of three to focus you on only mission critical things

2. **The trap of artificial urgency:** the tendency to label things as urgent even if they really aren't

    Solution: Work and life urgency filters that are specific to your situation and based on real criteria that allow you to objectively reconcile what is truly urgent and what isn't

3. **The trap of undefined boundaries:** the habit of trying to multitask and blend everything together with no clear lines in the sand

    Solution: Ruthless compartmentalization and line drawing but with consideration for the needs of coworkers, customers, and bosses so that you can reduce your need to multitask as well as mitigate fears of killing your career by drawing boundaries when others aren't

4. **The trap of no buffer zone:** the practice of not leaving any time for the unexpected and unanticipated

    Solutions: Simplify and reduce the things that aren't required, and formally implement a 50 percent buffer into everything you do

5. **The trap of constant triage:** the failure of allowing no time to think about what you really want and need in work and life (and how you are going to fulfill those wants and needs) because you are always fighting fires; in other words, the trap of living in a reactive state

    Solutions: Schedule thinking and planning time into your day every day, and adjust and broaden your approach to planning to include planning for family responsibilities, not just work responsibilities

6. ***The trap of chasing time:*** the tendency to focus on what's next instead of being in the moment and appreciating what you are doing right now

Solution: Commit to living in the moment, and use prompts during small life events to keep you from jumping into "next thing" thinking

7. **The trap of late nights getting it all done:** the pressure of trying to finish things when you are completely drained after exceedingly long days

    Solutions: Commit (or recommit) to the dawn patrol, and implement formal cutoff times at night

8. **The trap of forgetting about yourself:** the mistake of unintentionally making yourself the odd man out with all that work and life entailed

    Solution: Implement at least one restorative activity

Regularly tracking how you are doing with the eight traps is critical because old and new behaviors will enable or derail your attainment of your work-life vision. When you boil it all down to the real bottom line (the last time I'll say that in this book, only because the book is almost over), and for the sake of simplicity, all you really need to focus on is how effectively you are living your new work-life vision. Everything else—including the eight traps—are drivers of that vision.

After a year on this work-life balance journey, I reviewed my vision piece by piece and gave myself a grade.

1. **Specifically, what are my highest priorities for achieving quality time with my kids every week?**

    Big Ben: Take and pick him up from preschool on his designated days, do one full-day weekend outing with him every weekend, take him to speech/physical therapy each week to be part of his development, do an afternoon activity with him at least two days a week, read to him at night at least four days a week. Be present enough to play an active role in shaping his value and behaviors.

    MY GRADE: A (I was doing every one of these things.)

    Ivan the Tank: Play with him every day, read to him at night with

Big Ben, and evolve into the same things I do with Ben as Ivan gets older. Once he is done nursing, my role is going to ramp up a lot.

MY GRADE: A (Two for two felt pretty good. And I was ramping up my involvement with Ivan.)

<u>*Gabe*</u>*: Attend 75 percent of his soccer and volleyball games, work with him to prepare his college applications, take him on college tours, help him navigate the drama of high school, keep him focused on the most important things at a time when the most important things to a teenager might not be the most important things.*

MY GRADE: B+ (I was certainly making the best effort I could. Sometimes, dealing with teenage drama is mentally depleting. Most days, given all of the changes I had made to my work-life approach, I had the energy to do the hard work. Some days, I didn't. The positive difference here was that I had time allocated for it instead of trying to squeeze it in like I did before. Maybe that was what was working better here.)

<u>*Dani*</u>*: Simply be available to support her wherever she wants my support.*

MY GRADE: A (It's hard to give myself an A because by this age, Dani is pretty self-sufficient. But at least if she ever does have a need, I'll have time for it.)

2. **What specifically do I want to do with my wife each week that would make me feel like we had achieved quality time each week?**

Dinner or lunch once a week just to ourselves.

MY GRADE: B- (We do lunches once a week now. I'd like more. For the first time in a while, I feel like we might be able to make that happen.)

3. **What specifically do I need to do each week to ensure my health?**

Thirty minutes at the gym three times a week and some time every day for James-zone-out-nobody-is-in-my-face time.

MY GRADE: A- (I'm going three times a week to the gym, getting daily zone-out time, and even getting a little piano playing and *Far Side* reading in throughout the week, here and there. I'm not eating as well as I should, so that's going to be my next goal.)

4. **What specifically do I need to do to support my mom and sister?**

Get Big Ben and Ivan the Tank over to Grandma's and Aunt Sarah's house every other week.

MY GRADE: A+ (It's happening almost every other week, and it doesn't feel squeezed in.)

5. **What do I need to do every week to keep some form of contact with my lifelong friends?**

Call, text, and e-mail my friends each week even if we can't hang out much anymore. Find time once every few months to at least try to get together in person.

MY GRADE: C- (As well as I'm doing in the other areas, this one is still a problem. I'm just lucky to have good friends who continue to reach out to me in my state of MIA. This one needs work.)

6. **What do I need to do every week to successfully run my business in sustainability mode?**

Keep my current clients, do quality and timely work for them, and identify new work that makes sense for their business. Stay ahead of things and identify where current clients may begin to erode. Actively engage with my business network to identify new opportunities for work to supplement any potential revenue degradation. Define my bottom-end income threshold (in other words, that revenue level that I can't allow my business to fall below) and monitor attainment of it. Say "no" or "not now" to new client opportunities that stretch beyond keeping the business in sustainability mode and put me back into growth-at-all-costs mode. Minimize unnecessary business and financial expenses since I'm not growing the business right now. Continue writing weekly articles for business journals to continue to build my business reputation.

MY GRADE: B (Revenue numbers and projections certainly don't match the past eight years, so I keep reminding myself that my current work-life vision isn't designed for that to happen. Worrying about money does keep me up at night while I keep my eye on that bottom-end revenue threshold that I established. I also worry that I've swung the pendulum too far back the other way towards the family side, jeopardizing my business. The numbers are still good, though. Just different. Since I haven't operated like this in the last decade, it is taking a little getting used to. Because of that, I still have the tendency to accept client work that doesn't fit into the vision. It's a habit that brings in good revenue but stresses my work-life balance system. I'm doing well but still working on this one.)

If my math is correct, that's five As, three Bs, and a C-. It's not a perfect report card, but I'm feeling pretty good about my work-life balance. We'll need to compare report cards once you do yours (not that I'm competing or anything). I'm still tired a lot, but who wouldn't be. Being a dad to a toddler and a baby is physically exhausting. Being a dad to teenagers is an emotionally exhausting roller coaster fraught with euphoric highs and deep lows that you ride along with them. But I don't have to tell any of that to you. That's the parent role. On top of that, running a business requires constant attention and work, even if that business is not in growth mode right now. The good news—great news—is that I don't stress about where I'm going to fit in the most valued aspects of work and life anymore; they are built into my vision, which I'm sticking with. I'm not sure I'm ready to do a side-by-side work-life comparison showdown with Darryl from AP. As good as I feel about what I've done over the last year, I may never get to his lofty status. Then again, I'm no longer in any danger of getting sent down to the minor leagues. I've got sustainable guidelines to keep me on the work-life balance path and from falling off the wagon into old tendencies and habits.

Maybe the most crucial lesson I've learned while on this quest is that work-life balance is possible. And that's hopefully what you have picked up from this book. It isn't a mirage in the desert. Part of my journey was about finding work-life balance to solve my very real problems and hopefully giving you a methodology to help you with your own quest. The search was also about validating the belief I had that none of us were undertaking the impossible by seeking balance. We're not relegated to work-life blend, regardless of what a lot of people say. Though for some, work-life blend may be the right solution. My point is: there isn't only one way out of the work-life insanity. If I can pull it off and still maintain love in my heart for a neurotic dog and destructive rabbit, other dads can do it too. I'm no different than most dads out there. I'm not a psychologist. I don't meditate and may never meditate. I'm not a philosopher. I'm just a guy running a business who is happily married with four kids and a few pets. I'm just a dad with a lot of stuff going on—like every other dad out there—who tried to think a little differently about the imbalance problem. By some fluke of nature, a lot of it actually worked. I should probably thank my dad for everything I watched him do over the years. Thanks, Dad. And hopefully, you all feel a little better about your work-life balance situation—even the die-hard night dads out there.

A SYSTEM OF PROACTIVE SOLUTIONS
TO ENABLE SUSTAINABLE WORK-LIFE BALANCE

DEFINING YOUR WORK-LIFE BALANCE END GAME

Define priorities and trade-offs

YOU   *WORK*   *"LIFE"*

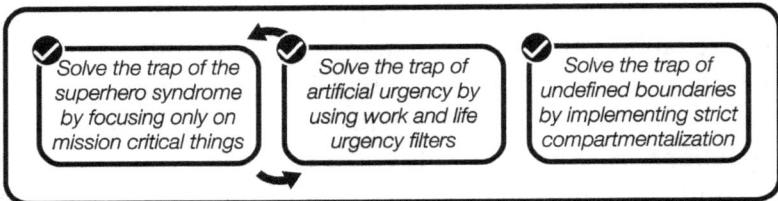

Solve the trap of the superhero syndrome by focusing only on mission critical things

Solve the trap of artificial urgency by using work and life urgency filters

Solve the trap of undefined boundaries by implementing strict compartmentalization

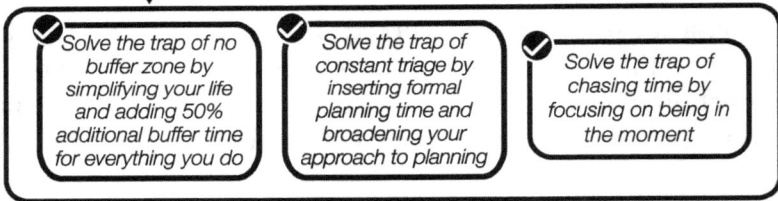

Solve the trap of no buffer zone by simplifying your life and adding 50% additional buffer time for everything you do

Solve the trap of constant triage by inserting formal planning time and broadening your approach to planning

Solve the trap of chasing time by focusing on being in the moment

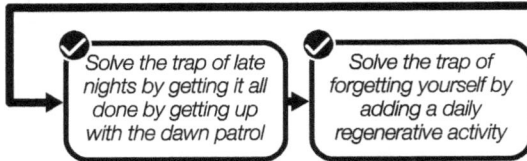

Solve the trap of late nights by getting it all done by getting up with the dawn patrol

Solve the trap of forgetting yourself by adding a daily regenerative activity

The Man in the Arena

"It is not the critic who counts; not the man who points out how the strong man stumbles, or where the doer of deeds could have done them better. The credit belongs to the man who is actually in the arena, whose face is marred by dust and sweat and blood; who strives valiantly; who errs, who comes short again and again, because there is no effort without error and shortcoming; but who does actually strive to do the deeds; who knows great enthusiasms, the great devotions; who spends himself in a worthy cause; who at the best knows in the end the triumph of high achievement, and who at the worst, if he fails, at least fails while daring greatly, so that his place shall never be with those cold and timid souls who neither know victory nor defeat."

Excerpt from President Theodore Roosevelt's landmark speech, "Citizenship in a Republic"

Acknowledgements

My wife, who inspires me every day to be the best husband and dad I can be.

My mom and dad, who have always been my role models and heroes in work and in life.

My sister, Sarah, who has always shown me what can be done with perseverance, regardless of the circumstances you are dealt.

Dani, Gabe, Ben, and Ivan, whose mere presence reminds me every day what is truly important in life as a dad or someone who is playing the role of dad to the best of his abilities.

My friend and talented illustrator, Todd Kale, who always seems to be thinking the same ridiculous thoughts I'm thinking, making collaborating on projects such as these easy and fun.

Kathy Burge, my editor, who is so good at her job that she, without fail, makes my work significantly better than it would have been without her.

The awesome team at Zilker Media, who I feel are my partners in crime and who always make me feel like their biggest author (even though we all know that I'm far from that).

About the Author

James Sudakow serves as the principal of CH Consulting, Inc., a boutique management and organizational effectiveness consulting practice he founded in 2010. He specializes in helping companies manage organizational transformation and create talent management strategies that improve business performance through people. Previously, he wrote *Picking the Low-Hanging Fruit . . . and Other Stupid Stuff We Say in the Corporate World*, a humorous illustrated corporate glossary that sheds an irreverent light on the numerous weird business buzzwords that have proliferated through the business world. *Picking the Low-Hanging Fruit* and Sudakow's business insights and articles have been featured in the *Chicago Tribune, Forbes, Fast Company*, Mic, *The Business Journals*, Lifehacker, Bustle, SiriusXM, *Psychology Today*, Arianna Huffington's Thrive Global, HR.com, *Entrepreneur*, Ladders, and more. He is also a contributing columnist to *Inc.* magazine. Before starting his own consultancy, Sudakow held leadership roles in several global multibillion-dollar organizations across the technology and health care industries. He lives in San Diego, California, with his wife and family. For more information, visit www.jamessudakow.com.

www.ingramcontent.com/pod-product-compliance
Lightning Source LLC
Chambersburg PA
CBHW030842210326
41521CB00025B/637